CELEBRATING DIFFERENCES

the work of bptw partnership

Contents

4 Introduction

5 Foreword

7 Chapter 1
Building Aspirations

27 Chapter 2
Masterplanning Change

83 Chapter 3
Raising Expectations

147 Chapter 4
Adapting for the Future

186 Timeline

188 Selected Bibliography

189 Acknowledgements

190 Index

Introduction

bptw partnership today is very different from the practice we sought to establish in its earliest years; shaped beyond recognition by 20 years experience and a wealth of understanding gained from the vast range of communities and developers we have had the privilege of working alongside.

Even so, our ethos and principles remain fundamentally unchanged: we aspire to design and build lasting, functional and aesthetically appealing homes that meet the specific needs of the communities in which we work.

Every scheme is different. We are proud that we have been able to change, improve and even transform the built environment to meet the unique social and design challenges of each of our projects.

At such a milestone in our practice's history, we welcome this opportunity to write about the work we have been involved in, the people that have allowed us to shape their homes and neighbourhoods, and the spirit of originality, enjoyment and co-operation of all those with whom we have had the pleasure of working.

Foreword

by Nick Raynsford MP

Celebrating Differences is a record of achievement. Over the past 20 years, bptw has developed and expanded its work and its impact in a range of different ways and locations. It has grown from modest beginnings into a large and successful practice which can rightly look back with considerable pride on what it has achieved. But this book is not just a record of the projects on which bptw has worked since 1988. It is also a testimony to the thoughtful and imaginative way in which bptw has approached some of the most important challenges facing our society.

Sustainability is rightly seen as fundamental to how we manage and develop our built environment, but it poses a complex challenge. We frequently tend to focus on specific aspects of sustainability, whether these be environmental, social or economic. Currently, for entirely understandable reasons, carbon reduction is afforded particular emphasis. But the real challenge for those who care about achieving sustainable outcomes rather than simply ticking boxes is to understand the inter-relationship of all the elements. Building new homes with high standards of energy efficiency is important, but not enough if the people who will live in them are left trapped by social exclusion. New developments that look striking on first viewing, may take on a very different appearance if they do not prove a practical and pleasant place in which to live and work. The current controversy on the future of the Robin Hood Gardens Estate in Poplar is a classic illustration of the conflicts which arise when architectural and social objectives are pulling in different directions.

It has been one of the key objectives of bptw from the outset to create places that not only look good but which work and which respond to the diverse needs of the people who will occupy and visit them. This calls for real sensitivity and understanding and a willingness to listen and learn from those who will live in and around the new buildings long after the opening celebrations.

Good design and architecture inevitably crystallises a vision in response to a brief at one point in time. But the outcome will be there long into the future when not just the vagaries of fashion, but also society's economic, social and environmental priorities will all have moved on. The truly successful and sustainable developments are those which are able to accommodate that process of change and which are not left looking increasingly incongruous and dysfunctional as a result of the passage of time.

It would be tempting providence to forecast that all bptw's projects will pass this very difficult test. But from my experience of the work of the practice over most of its existence I am confident that its legacy will continue to be seen in a very positive light. I feel honoured to have been asked to write this Foreword to bptw's twentieth anniversary publication, and I am proud and delighted to have such a committed, imaginative and successful practice based in my Greenwich and Woolwich constituency.

Building Aspirations

Set against a backdrop of economic volatility, an uncontrolled soar in property prices and widespread change in the legislature of social housing, Spring 1988 was not a perceptibly opportune time for the launch of new practice Bottomley, Palmer, Taylor & Wright, Architects and Quantity Surveyors.

A combined force of three young architects and a more experienced quantity surveyor, Mark Bottomley, Stephen Palmer, Roger Taylor and Alan Wright met working for Sampson Associates, and established the new practice in a two bedroom Victorian flat in Bethnal Green, reliant only on pooled personal finances, a range of experience and a collective desire to invest their efforts in meaningful, lasting and exemplary design.

Despite acquiring a significant amount of their prior experience from the commercial sector; Roger Taylor contributing over a decade of practice and invaluable industry knowledge in his role as former Assistant Chief Quantity Surveyor at the London Borough of Haringey in addition to his time at Sampson Associates, Palmer gaining a high technical knowledge from his time with Sheppard Robson, and all four on a series of large linked projects close to Old Street roundabout, there was little intention to concentrate efforts in this area.

Drawing instead on Alan Wright's sheltered housing work with Pollard Thomas Edwards Architects, his early academic influences, including Hans Scharoun, Alvar Aalto and Frank Lloyd Wright, Mark Bottomley's close-hand experience of his architect parents' pioneering social housing work, and the contemporary responses of established practices to the wider issues of housing and community regeneration, the newly formed practice began to focus attention on the increasingly prominent social housing sector.

A product of the Conservative administration's increasing zeal for social sector privatisation, heightened efforts to access the financial value of private investment and stock transfer in community housing and concurrent recognition of the widespread problems in the same arena, the issue of public housing conditions had risen steadily higher on the Thatcher government's political agenda. Addressing this, the Estate Action programme, launched by the Department of the Environment in 1985, was a significant marker of change.

Designed to help local authorities in England fund the "transformation of unpopular housing estates into places where people would want to live", the programme ostensibly addressed the more inherent problems of run-down social housing. Notably, beyond the implementation of physical change, Estate Action also made resources available for improvements in local housing management, tenure diversification, the attraction of private investment and opportunities for training and enterprise.

Transformation, however, was inevitably going to be hard to achieve. Founded in the post-war mass-production of low cost, low quality, high-rise housing and a backlog of overdue repairs and

Bishport Avenue, Bristol.

renovations, the sheer scale of the problems facing social housing had become an indomitable force. The capital investment available through the Estate Action Programme was perceptibly limited in comparison.

Although there were exceptions, residents of the some four hundred tower blocks erected in London in the sixties generally experienced a prevalent sense of social ostracisation as the post war vision of the urbane vertical community disintegrated around them. Victim to the realities of inadequate housing management and maintenance, many of the high-rise estates had become pockets of deprivation encompassing economic inactivity, high levels of crime, a lack of security and general urban decay.

Fundamental to this disintegration was the neglect of the streetscape; the failure to recognise the asset of open and welcoming neighbourhood space, and the security that communal propriety brought to shared land. Acknowledging this, it was glaringly obvious that any repair to the physical

Left: St George's Court at night
Right: St Patrick's Court: one of two high-rise buildings comprising bptw's first significant scheme.

or social fabric of these sites would have to incorporate the wider social, environmental and economic context if it was to have any success.

Responding to these issues, established architectural practices such as Levitt Bernstein, Hunt Thompson Associates and Phippen, Randall & Parkes, had started to adopt a more holistic approach to regeneration and the provision of community housing, notably, through their alignment with emerging housing associations within the increasingly prominent social sector. Contemporaneously, motivated by the way in which these specialised community schemes were able to knit into wider regeneration strategies, Bottomley, Palmer, Taylor & Wright began exploring similar design approaches.

Fittingly therefore, the practice's first significant scheme involving the structural strengthening and refurbishment of two structurally unsound local authority owned tower blocks, St George's & St Patrick's Court, in the London Borough of Waltham Forest, brought Bottomley, Palmer, Taylor & Wright directly alongside Hunt Thompson who, by separate appointment, were simultaneously selected to work on two blocks in the close vicinity.

Driven by the technical challenges posed by the scale of refurbishment and representatives of the large resident community group who would remain in occupation throughout the design and construction process, St George's & St Patrick's afforded the new practice invaluable experience in community consultation.

With over 50 flats in each tower block, and a responsibility to carry out both full internal refurbishment and structural strengthening to the building; resident backing was fundamental to the projects success.

Garnered through an exhaustive consultation process incorporating initial community meetings, door-to-door questionnaire surveys, newsletters and a resident steering committee, support for the project developed in tandem with the communities' involvement in the development process. This continued to evolve as the practice's partners, themselves learning over the course of the project, responded to resident feedback.

Manifesting itself in a show of overwhelming resident support, the successful consultation led the eventual refurbishment to become a genuine reflection of the aspirations of the St George's & St Patrick's community. Tellingly, the refurbished buildings were designed to restore the original brickwork on the external fabric, maintaining the aesthetic qualities that made these tower blocks popular for the residents in the first place.

Even the technical process became part resident led; the tenants having selected one of their preferred construction methods on the basis of on-site drilling sessions, organised by bptw to demonstrate the differences between the sound, impact and time-considerations of percussive and water-cooled drilling. Remarkably, the residents opted for the less prolonged but louder procedure which, perceived as less disruptive, demonstrated the community commitment to the refurbishment.

Given the prolonged nature of the project; the structural problems associated with strengthening large panel external construction and the full internal rewiring and bathroom and kitchen installations which took on average almost eight weeks inside each flat, the residents' willingness to persevere with the massive disruption in-and-outside of their homes, further testified to their full understanding of the reasoning behind the process and their confidence in the promised outcome. Including major landscaping, car park improvements and the design and fitting of new entrance halls and communal rooms on both tower blocks in addition to the overall refurbishment, the wait was, by all accounts, finally made worthwhile in December 1991.

While the completion of St George's & St Patrick's served to launch Bottomley, Palmer, Taylor & Wright as a practice of deserved repute, significantly helped by a ten page *Building Magazine* article featuring the two blocks as a high-rise success story, the practice's approach to the project also defined how they would continue to conduct business in the years going forward; responsibly, responsively and through consultation-led design.

Brought to the fore in the next major project, the strength of this approach would be augmented by the practice's renewal and repair of Bishport Avenue, five tower blocks in a declining estate in Hartcliffe, South Bristol. In a bid by the City Council to address the social problems fragmenting the estate's community, the buildings required full external refurbishment and significantly large amounts of landscape design in early 1992.

Having procured the scheme against competition from local architects in 1992, the consultation process saw Bottomley, Palmer, Taylor & Wright temporarily relocating to the Hartcliffe area to engage with the community they would be working for, and to receive first-hand, the residents' indictment of the community's experience of endemic joy-riding, prevalent substance misuse and the consequence of their estate being used as a re-homing ground for socially disassociated single male residents.

Conversely, the three intensive days spent completing over 250 door-to-door questionnaire interviews and engaging over 85 per cent resident involvement, also exposed a strong community fabric, an articulate expression of specific local need and overwhelming support for the design process, which would continue through to the end of the construction stages.

Attributable to its fulfilment of the residents' needs, the completed schemes success revealed itself in a landscape design in which it was physically impossible to joy ride, a humanised environment that enhanced the estates overall security, restructured entrances to the flats, protected existing and created new recreational space in the form of private gardens for each tower block and secure play areas outside the communal laundries which, despite deep-seated maintenance problems across the estate, remained an exceptionally well-cared for and much lauded source of community pride.

Testament to the individuals involved and the residents, contractors and builders responsible for the day-to-day logistical undertaking of the occupied refurbishment process, Bishport Avenue was a hugely consolidating experience for the practice. Underlining both the overarching need for contextual architecture and landscaping, the socially restorative impact of an improved streetscape

Top: Cranwood Street, a large mixed commercial development undertaken for Sampson Associates.
Bottom left and right: Avenue Road, Leytonstone, shown before and after refurbishment.

and the unique benefit of community involvement in designing for the social housing sector, the practice had firmly established their area of expertise.

Nevertheless, between the more landmark schemes the practice meanwhile continued to work on a range of smaller projects, including the conversion of a mews houses in Primrose Hill, refurbishment work on various London restaurants and the conversion of a North London synagogue to apartments. These projects not only contributed to the practice's financial stability but also broadened their design experience, client-base and wider understanding of mixed-use, residential needs and costs across the sectors. Indeed, brought to the practice by the contractors of the Waltham Forest tower blocks, the synagogue conversion was also a forerunner of bptw's characteristic close working with contractors and developers, demonstrating a trend that continues to be cultivated to the present day, with mutual benefits of developing greater understanding between designers and constructors.

Left: Finchley Methodist Church, post-refurbishment.
Right: Crank's Restaurant, Covent Garden: one of several restaurants refurbished by bptw, the redesign focussed on creating inviting dining interiors, crucially implemented within tight time schedules, minimising interruption to trade.

The freedom this afforded led neatly into the practice's appointment as masterplanners, quantity surveyors and lead designers for the extensive regeneration of the Woodpecker Neighbourhood in South London, specifically focussed on the Milton Court Estate. Involving the demolition of seven tower blocks, high-rise and low-rise refurbishment and the conversion of maisonettes and new-build housing, the practice's selection for the project was an appropriate reflection on their growing capacity as a practice. As articulated by the London Borough of Lewisham on appointing bptw for the project, it also reflected the sector's opinion that the practice could be relied upon to provide "community architecture as it needed to be delivered".

Growth in itself had brought fundamental change and by Autumn 1988, Bottomley, Palmer, Taylor & Wright had already outgrown Mark Bottomley's Bethnal Green flat. After a year renting studios in Kentish Town the practice moved to Greenwich in 1991 and went on to purchase a converted Mission Hall in East Greenwich two years later. As the practice changed size and direction, founding partner Stephen Palmer, retired in 1992 and Bottomley, Palmer, Taylor & Wright moved forwards under the name of BPTW Architects and Quantity Surveyors, subsequently evolving to bptw partnership reflecting the increased diversity of services offered by the practice.

In conjunction with the practice's focus on community engagement and transparency in design, internal communication became increasingly significant as staff numbers rose. Upholding the need for the design process to be enjoyable and rewarding for all involved, the partners displayed an early commitment to the development of a coherent, supportive and stimulating staff culture. Reflecting the success of this approach, the retention of the practice's employees spoke volumes.

Formally supplementing these efforts, the practice received a DTI grant dedicated to marketing, communications and business practice in 1991. Taking advantage of the sophisticated presentation training and promotion advice it provided, the still-small practice learnt to provide assured, convincing arguments for their own appointment above that of significantly more established practices.

Their confidence was justified. With a threefold increase in staff, increasing acclaim from the housing sector and the roots of what would develop into a lasting relationship with developing housing associations firmly in place, bptw partnership celebrated their fifth year of practice with direction, a growing reputation and a number of ambitious projects in the pipeline.

St George's & St Patrick's Court

bptw's first scheme of significance, the refurbishment and regeneration of St George's & St Patrick's Court, two structurally unsound tower blocks in the London Borough of Waltham Forest, afforded the fledgling practice an invaluable experience in community consultation and the opportunity to establish themselves as perceived 'regeneration specialists' in the rapidly developing social housing sector.

The outcome of a drive by the London Borough of Waltham Forest to undertake a survey of its stock of 44 high-rise tower blocks, revealing that five of these required refurbishing and structural improvement; bptw's successful bid to carry out this work led to their appointment on two of the identified buildings in autumn 1988.

Including St George's Court on the edge of Walthamstow, and St Patrick's, set into a sloping wooded site in Woodford Green, the two blocks required significant structural strengthening to counteract potential risks of progressive collapse, and general refurbishment and modernisation, which would include the installation of new water storage tanks, power circuit wiring and purpose made skirting trunking, upgraded heating and new kitchen and bathroom fittings. General improvements

Left: St George's Court, Walthamstow.
Opposite: St Patrick's Court, Woodford Green.

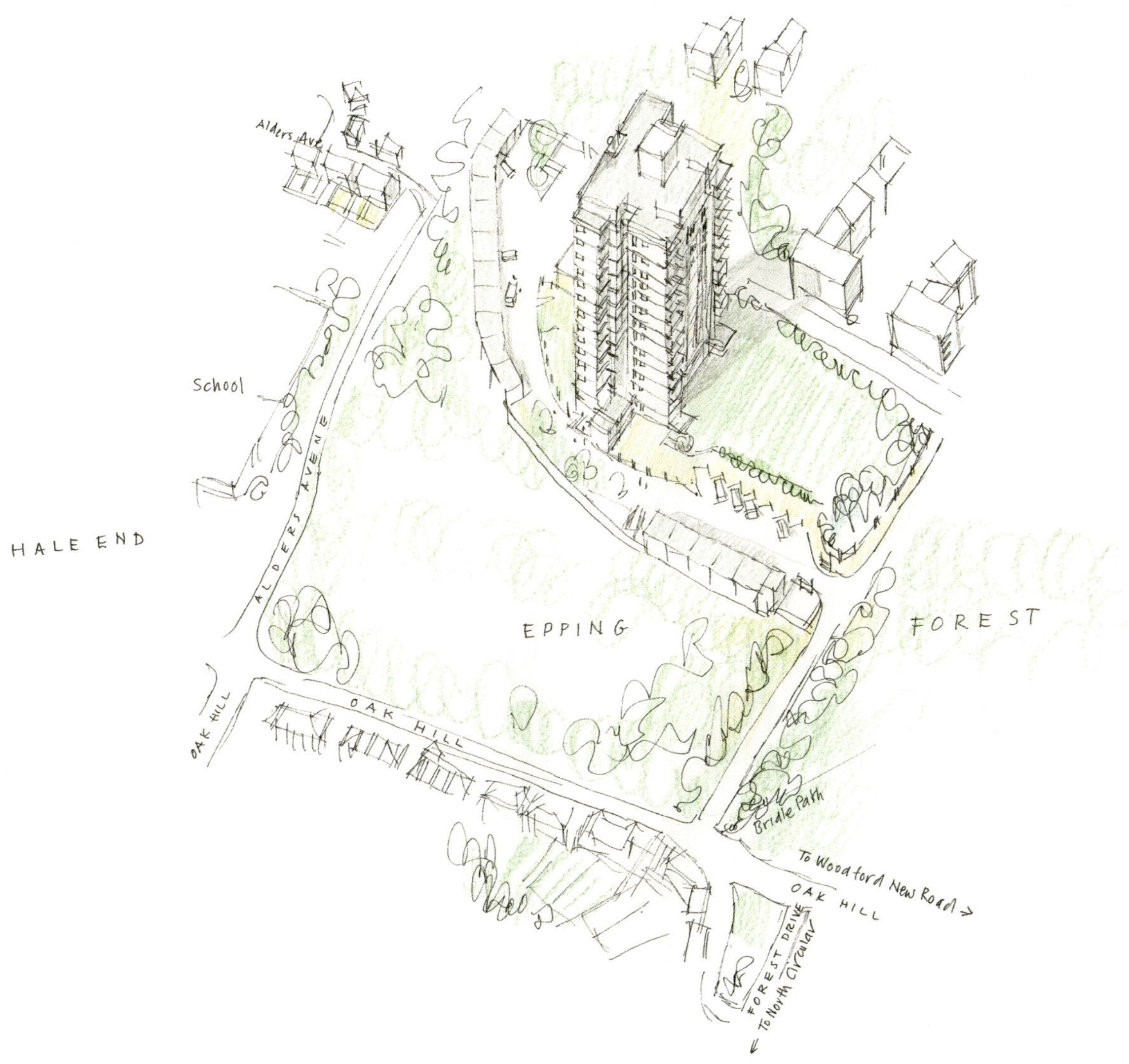

to the landscaping surrounding the building would also be carried out. Notably, by separate appointment, Hunt Thompson was simultaneously selected to work on two other blocks in the close vicinity.

Due to the technical challenges posed by the scale of internal refurbishment and the 50 flats in each tower block that would remain occupied throughout the design and construction process, the backing of the St George's & St Patrick's residents became fundamental to the project's success from the onset.

Initiating the residents' central involvement in the project, bptw carried out an exhaustive consultation process incorporating surveys of tenants' views on the blocks and how they felt the buildings could be improved. The results were subsequently presented at tenants meetings and options for improvements were outlined. Weekly design steering group meetings attended by representative groups from each block were used to develop these proposals further and remaining tenants were kept informed by regular newsletters giving details of any decisions made.

Epitomising the extent of the residents' direction of the regeneration process, tenants were even able to select between certain construction methods for the refurbishment, determined on the basis of on-site drilling sessions, organised by bptw to demonstrate the differences between the sound, impact and time-considerations of percussive and water-cooled drilling. Similarly, following the completion of a preliminary contract in early 1989, an exhibition was held in the first newly refurbished flat to demonstrate the effect of the proposed internal works and to provide the opportunity for tenants to choose their preferred style of kitchen unit and kitchen and bathroom floor coverings from a range of samples. Thereby, manifesting itself in a show of overwhelming resident support, the successful consultation led the eventual refurbishment plan to become a genuine reflection of the aspirations of the St George's & St Patrick's residents.

Once the refurbishment work was underway, the residents' willingness to persevere with the considerable disruption in-and-outside of their homes, especially the internal rewiring and bathroom and kitchen installations which took on average almost eight weeks inside each flat, further testified to their confidence in the promised outcome. Significantly, the contractor, J Hodgson Ltd, appointed tenant liaison officers to each block to keep tenants notified of access requirements and to discuss any problems arising during the works. Refuge cabins were also provided as a means of allowing the residents to escape from the immediacy of the disruption.

Work on the external fabric of the tower blocks was ultimately completed in January 1991. Aesthetically, the outward appearance of the two blocks appeared revitalised but largely unchanged; a direct result of the residents' request to retain and reclad the buildings with brickwork similar in appearance to the original blocks. Structurally however, with the provision of thermal insulation on external walls, improved double glazed aluminium windows and purpose-made precast slab edge cladding panels, in addition to the installation of stainless steel structural strengthening angles, the building was vastly improved.

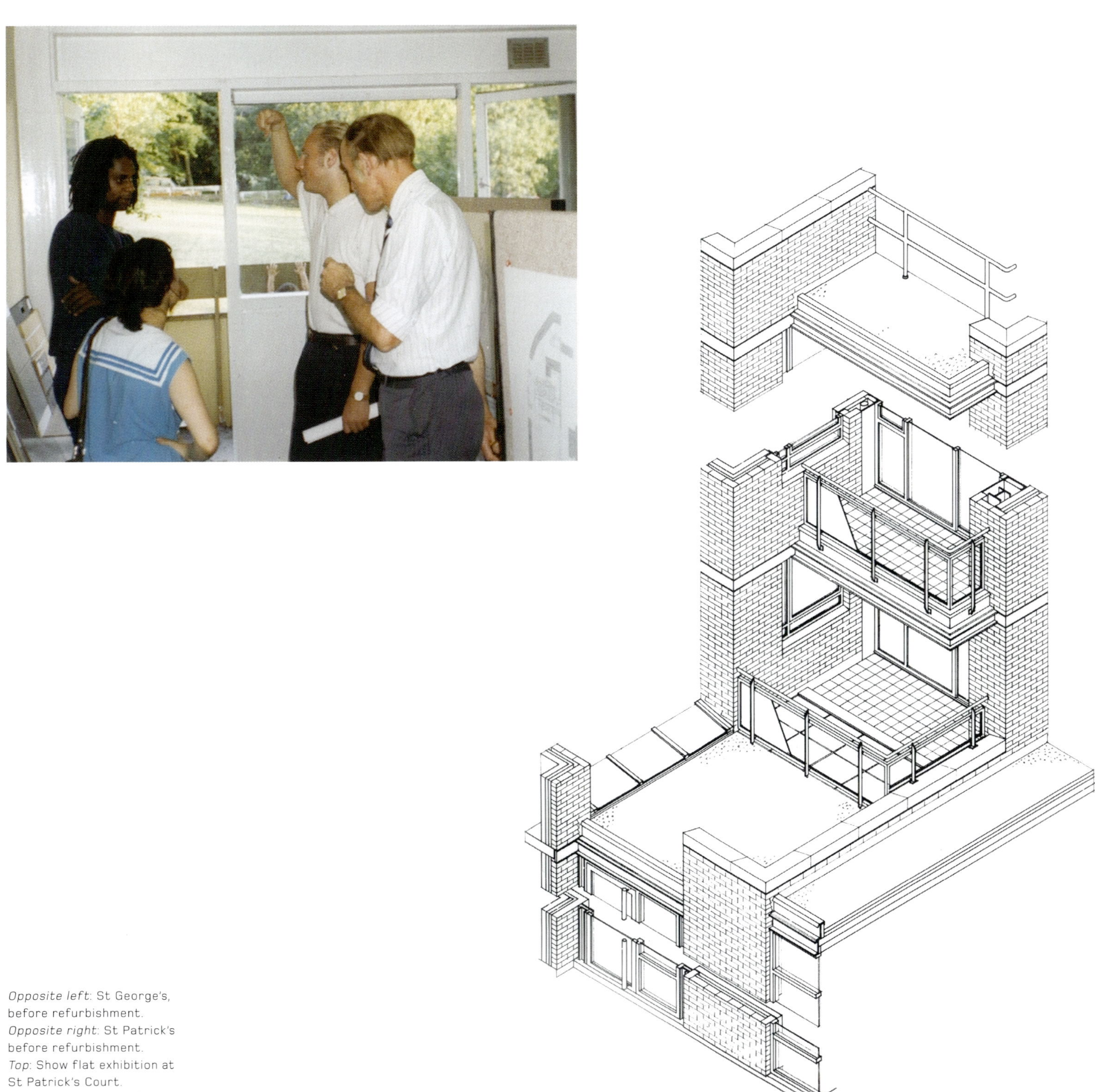

Opposite left: St George's, before refurbishment.
Opposite right: St Patrick's before refurbishment.
Top: Show flat exhibition at St Patrick's Court.
Right: Axonometric of the new ground floor extension and balconies.

The project was subsequently brought to a conclusion with the completion of communal facilities and the landscaping of the buildings immediate surrounding; involving, on St George's Court, the removal of underused garages and their replacement with green space and landscaped car parking areas. Tenant stores were constructed and the area around the blocks that had not been used was converted into private garden space for the residents. Significantly aiding the revitalised sense of community, ownership and resident pride in the two blocks, bptw also provided new enlarged entrance halls and common rooms in the ground floor of each block.

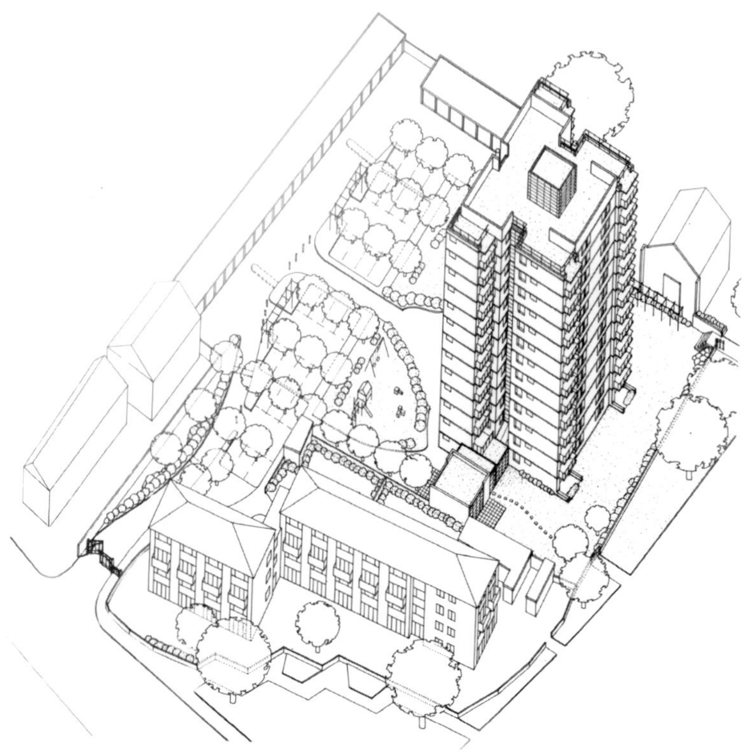

Completed in its entirety in December 1991, the success of the St George's & St Patrick's refurbishment subsequently played a significant role in launching bptw as a practice of deserved repute. Helped in no small part by a ten page *Building Magazine* article featuring the project as a sector-wide high-rise success story, the project also came to define the way in which bptw would be perceived as responsible and responsive consultation-led community architects from their earliest days in practice.

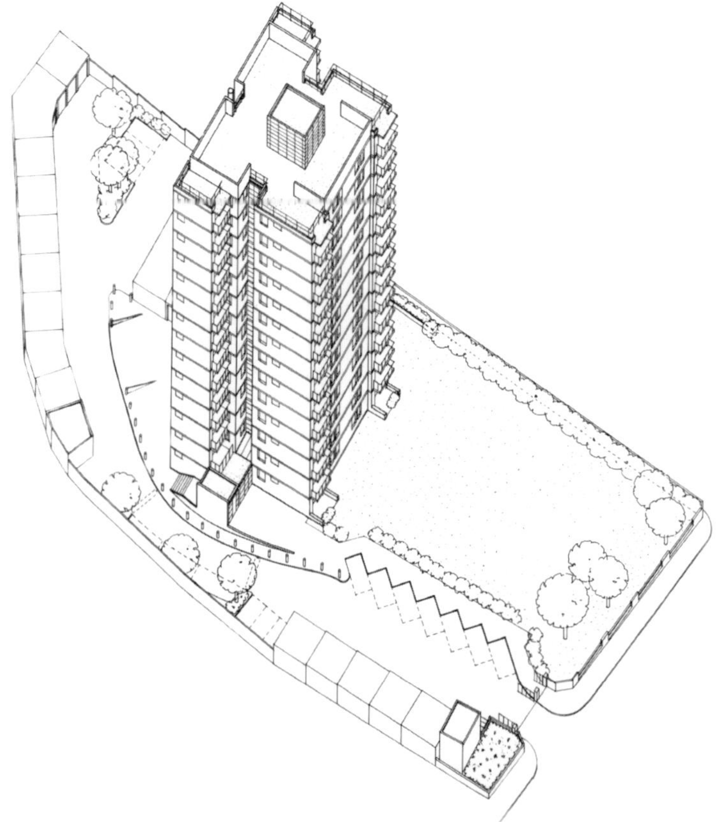

Opposite top: Aerial view of St George's showing proximity to neighbouring maisonettes and landscaped car parking to the north of the building.
Opposite bottom: Aerial view of St Patrick's highlighting generous landscaping to the front of the tower block.
Top left: Completed view of St George's Court, highlighting the private external space and play area.
Top right: St Patrick's Court and surrounding landscaping, post-refurbishment.
Bottom: St George's Court, mid refurbishment.

Left: Completed view of St Patrick's, focussing on newly glazed aluminium windows and balconies.
Opposite top: Refurbished tower block entrances leading through to newly created internal communal space.
Opposite bottom: View of entrance typical of each tower block prior to refurbishment.

Bishport Avenue

Supported by a high profile *Building Magazine* article establishing bptw's reputation as high-rise regeneration specialists within the housing sector, and wide acclaim gained from bptw's successful refurbishment of the St George's & St Patrick's tower blocks in the London Borough of Walthamstow; a well-received cold call to Bristol City Council resulted in the practice's invitation to tender for appointment on an Estate Action options appraisal contract. Subsequently procuring the scheme against competition from local architects, bptw were selected to provide the planning, on-site design work and contract administration services for the £12 million refurbishment and regeneration of five 11 storey tower blocks within a declining estate in early 1992.

Located in south Bristol, the residents of Bishport Avenue and the surrounding Hartcliffe community were experiencing the impact of ubiquitous social and economic decline as a result of the relocation of two primary local employers in the late 1980s, the increasing prevalence of anti-social behaviour, endemic joy-riding and substance-abuse and the widespread misuse of the community's public realm. Recognising the role of Hartcliffe's aging housing stock within this degeneration, the City Council's decision to fund the extensive landscaping and renewal and repair of Bishport Avenue was a significant bid to address the wider social problems fragmenting the estate's community.

Underlining the overarching need for contextual architecture and landscaping, and the necessity of resident involvement in creating socially restorative solutions for their own community, bptw subsequently approached the design and construction for the tower block refurbishment with an extensive consultation process, temporarily relocating the entire bptw office to Bristol to complete the initial consultation firsthand.

Eventually engaging over 85 per cent resident involvement, the three days spent completing over 250 door-to-door questionnaire interviews not only provided a vital insight into the residents' main tensions and concerns surrounding the neighbourhood in its existing condition, and their aspirations for the area following its redevelopment; but the process also exposed a strong community fabric, an articulate expression of specific local need and overwhelming support for the design process, which would continue through to the end of the construction stages.

Although the internal refurbishment works concentrated on one tower at a time, minimising the disruption to the

Opposite left: Access route to the tower blocks from Bishport Avenue.
Opposite right: Bishport Avenue before refurbishment.
Above: bptw's proposal for Bishport Avenue, Bristol.

community as much as possible; given that the residents remained in occupation for the duration of the project, this support would prove critical to the ease with which the significant design improvements were carried out. Contractor, Connaught Construction, also provided an on-site office and resident liaison officer to help support residents while work was underway.

Including the refitting of bathrooms and kitchens, and the fitting of double glazed windows in each of the apartments, internal enhancements on the tower blocks also incorporated the provision of new entrance halls and the introduction of a conservatory and communal area in each tower block. The restructured entrances were particularly significant for their role in heightening the security of each block, increasing the level of resident interaction and allowing for a greater sense of belonging within the neighbourhood.

Undertaken in a second phase, the design improvements to the external elevations of towers served to enhance the original architectural features and included the construction of new entrance canopies and balconies. Brick features on the first floors of the building, with insulated render over-cladding used on the upper levels.

Simultaneous to the refurbishment underway on the tower blocks, bptw worked in tandem with Bristol City Council's landscape architects to develop the existing public space, introducing in the process improved lighting and security features to deter criminal activity and vandalism, and re-orientating thoroughfares to reveal a landscape design in which it was physically impossible to joy ride. New recreational spaces were also created in the form of private gardens for each tower block and secure play areas outside the communal laundries which, uniquely characteristic of the Bristol area, remained well-used and exceptionally well-cared for within the community.

Opposite left: Development of the public space involved improved lighting and an increase in the proximity between the residents' access routes and the public realm to deter criminal activity and vandalism.
Opposite centre: Illustrating the private green space created for each building, protected through sensitive fencing and careful planting.
Opposite right: The new lobby: the design focussed on the use of bold colour, effective lighting and the use of full length glazing, increasing the openness and security of the entrance area.
Top: View of the new entrances and extensively restructured access routes to one of the five Bishport Avenue tower blocks.
Bottom: Bishport Avenue, Hartcliffe, Bristol, post-completion.

Masterplanning Change

Having developed strength as a vibrant, independent new practice, the new impetus of urban policy in the mid-1990s paradoxically saw bptw partnership spend the considerable part of the remainder of their first decade working largely in collaboration with other organisations; architects, contractors and developers; across the housing sector. A defining characteristic of urban policy between 1991 and 1998, and a sign of the pulling together of interest groups towards more holistic regeneration, this extensive partnership work would prove fundamental to bptw's development and served to create a base for several lasting relationships that would have a pivotal influence in the shape of the practice's future.

One of several factors driving this change, the Single Regeneration Budget Challenge Fund was launched by Michael Heseltine, Secretary of State for the Environment, in April 1994 and followed on the back of City Challenge, the first competition for resources through annual bidding rounds entered by partnerships. Encouraged by the earlier system's ability to galvanise different partners into collaboration, the housing-specific Single Regeneration Budget (SRB) sought to streamline this mechanism further, spurring partnerships across the public, private and community sectors and increasing the eligibility, range and flexibility of regeneration funding.

Initiated by Heseltine's conviction in the inter-relatedness of problems such as poor housing, low education and training standards, crime and a poor environment, the SRB Challenge Fund was also seen as a channel through which the multi-faceted issues of local need, wealth creation and economic competitiveness would be addressed by the diversity of collaboration.

However, given the lack of fixed policy boundaries, bids were notably varied in range. Against a high standard of competition, the majority of successful bids received assistance of less than £10 million and sought to bring about highly localised regeneration on single thematic schemes. Only a small minority were awarded sufficient funds for large scale multiple objective projects, many of them inevitably in London.

Among them, was the £59.9 million Peckham Partnership project, the masterplanning, consultation and design for which was led by bptw in partnership with Pollard Thomas Edwards architects. Supplemented by an additional £200 million from a wide range of partners the project involved the regeneration of five estates in Peckham, South London, and would bring to the fore bptw's capacity for delivery, the practice's collaborative strength and the wide ranging project experience gleaned from the earlier years of the practice.

Reinforcing bptw's proposal for the redevelopment of the Peckham estates, the regeneration of Milton Court was among the most significant of these projects. A high density, physically isolated and perceived 'intractably bad' estate, bptw were initially appointed by the London Borough of Lewisham to carry out feasibility and cost appraisal work on the Woodpecker development. Encouraged by the young practice's increasing familiarity with the local population, their readiness to carry out

Lime Tree House, phase one, Peckham.

a full consultative programme on the estate, and the availability of Estate Action funding for the neighbourhood, council officers sought bptw's assistance preparing bids for funding for the full regeneration of the estate.

Leading the project as masterplanner, architect and quantity surveyor throughout the design and construction process, from 1993 bptw was also uniquely managing the project from an on-site office. An immediate point of contact for the residents, this in itself exacerbated the reliance of the project on the success of extensive resident consultation and the interpretation and surmounting of the more inherent problems facing the Woodpecker Neighbourhood; partly attributable to the failure of the mono-tenure local housing mix, partly to the misuse of the original architectural structure; all, however, were characterised by widespread anti-social behaviour, heightened levels of crime and pervading social deprivation.

Significantly, as important as the holistic and integrated solutions appeared, the emphasis based on remedying the Woodpecker Neighbourhood's built environment represented 80 per cent of the residents' concerns, the non-physical and socio-economic issues only the remaining 20 per cent. Responding to this, and the highly vocalised desire for a return to the traditional virtues of street architecture, bptw completed an options appraisal process that clearly established the case for the complete demolition of seven of the blocks, and the refurbishment of Hawke Tower, the eighth and the only one retained as it had recently benefited from the installation of a concierge system.

The neighbourhood was steadily reshaped to recover the notion of an active and safe communal street frontage, with residents remaining in occupation throughout. Eventually transforming one of the most problematic estates in London, the Milton Court Masterplan served to highlight the absolute necessity of good design as an indispensable element of comprehensive estate regeneration, and exemplified the quantifiable reduction of deprivation of exactly the kind the Single Regeneration Budget Challenge Fund sought to achieve.

Similarly augmenting their commitment to strategic refurbishment and redesign, bptw were also tasked with the regeneration of Handcroft Road Estate in the London Borough of Croydon in 1994.

Built to conventional Radburn principles, the hard-to-manage underground car parks, raised access and play decks, single corridor features and concealed passageways of the 21 block estate had become unfortunate conduits for crime and pervasive anti-social behaviour. Addressing this, bptw's chief focus for the refurbishment of Handcroft Road was the improvement of the estate's existing streetscape. Based on consultation feedback regarding the residents' main concerns, the designs involved blocking 'no-go' alleyways and corridors and replacing every third garage with ground level entrance halls that faced streets and open landscaping, visible play areas and increased opportunity for community interaction.

The outcome was a success and in conjunction with the efforts of the local authority, the design improvements and partnership between residents, housing managers and service providers enabled the estate to be transformed into a considerably more welcoming, clean and safer environment with new links to the wider community. The estate's structural vulnerability and the complexity of the improvements required to be made to the site also represented a period of rapid expansion and diversification in the practice's design capabilities, and was an indicator of bptw's future capacity for housing design on a larger scale.

Appropriately therefore, 1994 saw bptw's appointment by Alfred McAlpine as post-planning executive architect to implement designs initially drawn up by Hunt Thompson on Oliver Close and Chingford Hall; two new housing developments for Waltham Forest Housing Action Trust that afforded the practice their first major new build scheme, and established their authority to offer these services to future clients.

Opposite left: The newly refurbished entrance to Hawke Tower, the only original tower block retained at Milton Court.
Opposite right: Brick overcladding to refurbished maisonettes at Milton Court.
Top left and right: Illustrating the return to traditional street architecture which formed the core of the neighbourhood's redesign.

Supplementing this were a number of additional, smaller projects which also served to widen the practice's design experience and reputation within the social housing sector. These included Clinton House, a new-build terrace scheme of 11 family homes in Deptford, South London, which involved the practice's close working with the local Beaver Housing Society; Bentham Court in Islington, representing bptw's first project with Circle Anglia Housing Association and comprising of the refurbishment of above-shop flats, and the redevelopment of large parts of the Shepway Estate

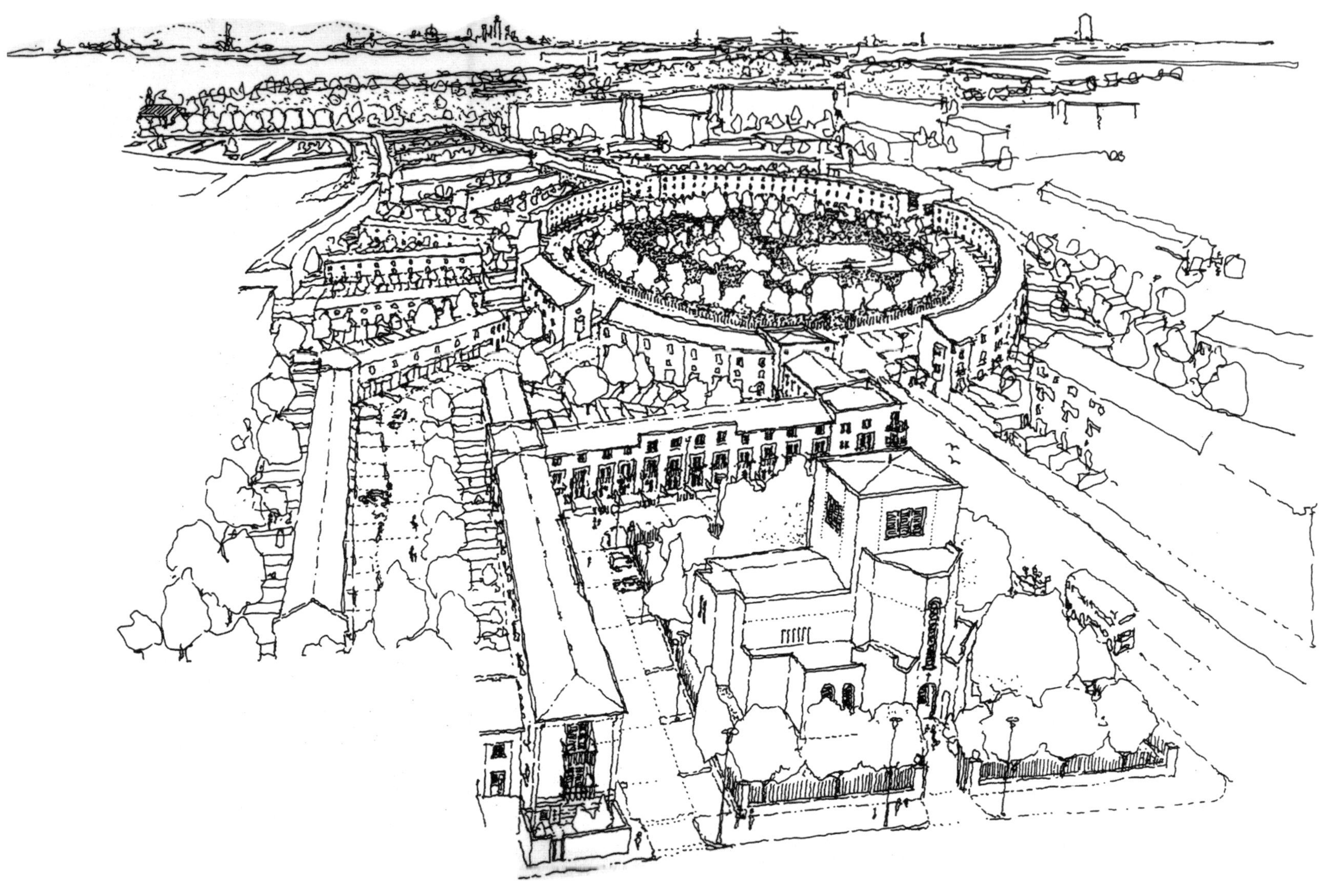

Above: Sketch of the original Peckham Partnership design for the Five Estates.
Opposite: View of Lime Tree House from north.

in Maidstone; a significant consultation project and an apt precursor to the practice's later work with the stock-transfer ballot consultations.

Accommodating this increase and diversification of workload, bptw gained a number of new appointees and their varying strengths allowed the practice to significantly widen its scope in terms of sector knowledge, methodology and process development.

Among them were a number of the practice's future partners. First appointed in 1991 and 1993 respectively, Robert Silcock and Dave Welsh brought wide-ranging industry understanding and extensive technical knowledge to the practice overall.

With equal effect, Mark Waite joined in 1996 to lead information management and to oversee the exponential growth in the practice's technological business solutions. Having already acquired two CAD workstations used to produce simple plans and schedules, bptw were progressive with their use of information technology and under Mark Waite's increasing supervision, the period leading to Peckham Partnership's completion saw the almost complete relegation of traditional drawing boards in favour of modern computer-based systems.

Concurrently, Andrew French, 1995, added high profile architectural experience and would become the first non-founding partner in January 1999, while Anna Parkinson, 1994, and Andy Heath, 1997 contributed a range of architectural skills and influences that would feed directly into a number of practice-defining projects, even as the Peckham Partnership work was underway.

Lime Tree House, bptw's first elderly person's residential project was among these. Grounded in the practice's social ethos, design proposals focussed on enhancing social engagement and the connection between the facility's internal space and the outside community, while addressing the need to provide a co-existing sense of community and independent living for the elderly residents of the sheltered care environment.

Keen to maximise the use of natural light and the corner location of the site, bptw arranged the building to front onto two streets creating an enclosed landscape garden, effectively a communal 'garden room', with the specific intention that it should overlook the neighbouring street in addition to the residential home's private gardens. Incorporating large sliding screens that opened directly onto the outside, it enabled residents of Lime Tree House, regardless of mobility, to interact with activity taking place outside the facility and transformed the quality of their relationship with the public and private realm.

Underlining the longstanding success of this scheme, bptw were subsequently invited in 2004 to return to Lime Tree House to design an extension for the residential home, which, following feedback and requests from residents and staff at the home, adopted a similar design concept to the original work undertaken almost a decade earlier.

Although unique in its capacity as the practice's first foray into the specialist care sector, now an area of particular interest for bptw, the project synonymously reflected the way in which housing specialisms would become assimilated within the mainstream of the practice; avoiding the division of specialist groups and the separation out of function and design while safeguarding bptw's overarching social principles.

Following their appointment on Lime Tree House, the practice also drew on Anna Parkinson's experience of sustainability-led design to take on Mabley Green, an environmentally-focussed project based on the incorporation of renewable energy sources and energy efficient design solutions for Circle 33 Housing Trust. Involving two pairs of family houses and the integration of solar water heating and rainwater recycling features, it was contemporaneously one of the most advanced sustainability schemes in the residential sector; remarkable in terms of technological innovation, the client's progressiveness, and the opportunity it afforded bptw, a decade prior to the influx of statutory-led environmental requirements, to establish their credentials as a forward thinking practice at the centre of the growing sustainability debate.

This willingness to endorse and implement progressive change also served to underline the shared aspirations of bptw's expanding senior management team, reassuringly highlighting the future partners' commitment to the founding ethos and reinforcing the practice's aim to provide responsive and responsible solutions to urban living, in accordance with social and political change.

Contextualising these objectives, in the same year bptw celebrated a decade in business, 1998 saw the release of *Rethinking Construction*, a definitive report from the Construction Task Force commissioned by then Deputy Prime Minister, John Prescott, and led by Sir John Egan. Under instruction to analyse and apply the experience of radical change and improvement of other sectors for the guidance of the UK construction industry, the final report highlighted five key drivers of change: committed leadership, a client-focussed approach, integrated processes and teams, a quality driven agenda and commitment to people. These were, notably, a series of principles that bptw had adopted since its earliest days of practice.

Thereby, already compliant with the report's demand for the industry to set ambitious targets, effective measurements of performance and above all, open partnerships with communities, residents and stakeholders across the sector. The philosophy underlined by *Rethinking Construction* also reinforced the credence of bptw's close engagement with local authorities, housing associations and developers as they continued to broaden their design capability.

The Charlton Triangle scheme, incidentally bptw's first major project in the London Borough of Greenwich, particularly reflected the continuation and strengthening of this relationship. Involving the stock transfer and regeneration of four separate estates in the Charlton area, bptw were enlisted in 1999 by Family Housing Association to form a reputable community regeneration team, established to facilitate a bid for the transfer of the Charlton Triangle housing stock under the Estate Renewal Challenge Fund (ERCF).

Successor of the Estate Action Programme, the Conservative-introduced Estate Renewal Challenge Fund was created in 1995 to fund the transfer of run-down, often negative value urban council housing to new landlords, particularly local housing associations, who would be able to raise additional private finance to purchase and improve council properties. Crucially however, the scheme was wholly reliant on community support, requiring the full espousal of the existing council tenants for the transfer to take place.

Central to btpw's understanding of this process was the practice's appointment to carry out extensive refurbishment on Edrich House, a tower block in Stockwell, London Borough of Lambeth, that was being managed by Hyde Housing Association and subsequently transferred from local authority ownership to Hyde. Not only a challenging refurbishment task involving the restructuring of the communal entrances, ventilation systems and the overall enhancement of the environmental balance of the building, the project was also a precursor to the stock transfer of the wider Stockwell neighbourhood under the ERCF programme, which, following widespread consultation and the eventual vote of approval from local tenants, saw bptw become lead masterplanners for the regeneration of Stockwell's Studley Estate housing stock; a project which notably coincided with the 1997 national election and the subsequent appointment of the new Labour administration.

Opposite top: Mabley Green, 1999. Sustainable housing development of two houses incorporating photovoltaic panels, heat recycling and grey water recycling. *Opposite middle*: Charlton Church Lane. *Opposite bottom left and right*: Charlton Triangle, post-refurbishment. Showing the redeveloped external landscaping and secured pedestrian entrances for each of the housing blocks.

Top: Aerial view concept sketch of the Studley Estate in Stockwell, South London.
Bottom: Masterplan of the Studley Estate.
Opposite: Edrich House, Stockwell.

Significantly, despite Labour's longstanding reluctance to condone the transfer of social housing from local authority control, the unobtainable expenditure levels required to bring council housing up to standard, and the prioritising of public funding for education and health over deteriorating housing stock, swiftly resulted in the new government's pragmatic decision to identify with the stock-transfer agenda. Subsequently, the inherited ERCF programme, as the only feasible way of accessing the resources needed to modernise and improve council housing, remained fundamentally unchanged. Only in the second year of government, realising that stock transfer had largely taken place in the least deprived local areas, did the context of the policy begin to shift to prioritise regeneration and housing improvements in more disadvantaged areas.

In this context, brought in following a previously unsuccessful funding bid by the local authority, Family Housing Association drew on their high reputation in regeneration and on bptw's forte for consultation and community design, initially to convey the benefits of the proposals for the transfer in control of their council-owned homes to the newly established Charlton Triangle Homes Housing Association, a subsidiary of Family Housing Association, and, further to the success of the ballot, to help provide extensive refurbishment, regeneration and new build design services across the four estates.

In realising this aim, the project eventually became an exemplary model of successful stock transfer. Determined to involve local residents in vital decisions over the shaping of the transfer plans, and post-regeneration, in the genuine community governance of the area, each home was visited a minimum of three times in advance of the ballot. Successively, tenant liaison officers were in place throughout the duration of the refurbishment process and a number of residents' groups, concentrating on issues such as education, employment or diversity, were established to create opportunities for community development.

More quantifiably, high quality refurbishment of individual homes, including the basic redesigning of kitchens, bathrooms, windows and entrances, in addition to more extensive structural repair work, was carried out on nearly 1,000 homes across the four estates and the project was a publicly acknowledged success as a design solution for affordable homes and improved standards of housing in South London.

However, over the course of its five years, the Charlton Triangle scheme also posed a number of challenges to the practice. Characteristic of the reliance of Estate Renewal Challenge Fund schemes on the pre-transfer condition of local authority housing, fundamental problems inherent in the existing housing stock led to an increase of necessary repairs expenditure for the project. Similarly, plans around the viability of refurbishing and retaining the original buildings surrounded the redevelopment of Coutts House, an 11 storey housing block on a contaminated, former quarry site on Charlton Church Lane. Restricted to building off the original foundations, agreement was eventually reached to redevelop the site with new housing comprising a mix of flats and family housing.

Signalling the near-completion of the full stock transfer process, in addition to the early foundations of bptw's delivery of new-build homes, approval for the last phase of the Charlton Triangle project coincided with the final stages of work on the Peckham Partnership scheme.

Further to its achievement of Single Regeneration Budget funding in 1995, the scheme, involving the masterplanning, consultation and design for the regeneration of over 3,000 homes across five estates in Peckham, represented a step change for bptw.

Contemporaneously the fifth most deprived ward in the UK and emblematic of the breakdown of the failed post-war mono-tenured social housing, the issues of social decline, criminality and deprivation to be dealt with in Peckham were largely similar to the inherent physical and socio-economic problems of schemes such as Milton Court, and Handcroft Road Estate, yet due to their sheer scale, were considerably harder to overcome.

Originally in competition against more cautious proposals from two alternative consortia advocating the wide scale refurbishment of the area, the winning masterplan proposed, in line with residents' aspirations for their neighbourhood, the complete redevelopment of the five estates. A perceptibly contentious vision, the practice was required to provide evidence of overwhelming tenant support for their proposal before the final masterplan was eventually implemented.

Thereby, from the onset the Peckham Partnership project provided the Peckham community with a decisive voice and responsibility over the future of their own public realm. Major public exhibitions generated widespread interest and a huge wave of opinion from residents who had traditionally been given little room for expression. Meanwhile, organised visits to alternative housing developments helped the community develop a more complete understanding of the architects' proposals for the Peckham estates and allowed for the mutual exchange of aspirations for the community. An integral part of SRB funding, which by the time of the 1997 election was established as the key regeneration programme in England, the implementation of the Peckham Project also incorporated a strong socio-economic programme, providing opportunities for vocational training over the course of the construction process and educational and community support for local schools.

Eventually, following an envisaged seven year programme of development, the Peckham Partnership's ambitious ideals were, on the whole, successfully realised. The density of the five estates was significantly reduced, over 2,000 high quality mixed-tenure homes were provided, and above all, it was recognised for its new-found ability to function as a neighbourhood; a basic precept of urban living that had previously eluded the community.

The regeneration of the urban realm focussed on a return to public squares and defined streets that drew on successful Victorian streetscapes to create a natural sense of communal ownership over the neighbourhood. Similarly, the phased decant process enabled homes to be dispersed in small groups across the area; significantly allowing for the unprecedented introduction of private sale homes in what was formerly the worst part of the estate and leading to an overall re-organising of the area in terms of localism and cosmopolitanism. Combined with the provision of three large new parks, the lessening of the contrast between the Peckham estates and the more desirable Camberwell neighbourhood adjacent made considerable progress in tackling the wider causes of social and economic decline. Tangible rises in local property prices posed a direct challenge to assumptions regarding sales values in the area, specifically opposing the perception of the neighbourhood as a homogeneously fallible economic entity.

Thereby, Peckham became bptw partnership's first multi-award winning scheme, firmly establishing the practice's track record in the production of responsible new-build developments that successfully reconciled traditional community-focussed design with a forward thinking multi-tenured approach. Creating new precedents in terms of the professional relationships established between the architectural partnership, contractors, developers and local housing associations over the course of the project, it would also remain a lasting testament of bptw's ability to form successful collaborations that would achieve tangible results in terms of physical, social and economic change.

This success in itself inevitably brought a further expansion of the staff team and unavoidably, another series of office relocations. Acknowledging the increasing strength of their local roots, the practice remained in Greenwich, and in 1998 moved in to offices at Hilton's Wharf which remains their current home to this day.

Gaumont House, Peckham High Street. Replacing the well-known Peckham Bingo Hall, this redevelopment provided bptw with the opportunity to create a new residential landmark and contribute to the ongoing regeneration of the area after the redevelopment of the five estates.

Milton Court

Initially appointed by the London Borough of Lewisham to carry out feasibility and cost appraisal work for the refurbishment of Milton Court; a perceived 'intractably bad' housing estate; the local authority later sought bptw's assistance preparing the framework proposals for the complete regeneration of the neighbourhood under the Estate Action funding programme in 1992. The application was successful and following a competitive bidding process, bptw were appointed as masterplanners, quantity surveyors and lead designers for the extensive regeneration of the Milton Court Estate.

Formerly comprised of eight tower blocks, a range of high- and mid-rise buildings and maisonettes, Milton Court formed an integral part of the Woodpecker Neighbourhood situated in New Cross, South London. Combining an economically disillusioned mono-tenured population and the propensity for the post-war architectural structure to be socially misused and poor housing management, the neighbourhood was frequently translated as a byword for a difficult, costly to maintain and hard-to-let estate, prone to crime, drugs, anti-social behaviour and violence. With the objective for the £50 million regeneration project combining the Estate

Left: Milton Court, London Borough of Lewisham.
Opposite: The Woodpecker Neighbourhood, before refurbishment.

Action Programme's aim to "transform unpopular housing estates into places where people would want to live", with the London Borough of Lewisham's aspiration to introduce "community architecture as it needed to be delivered", bptw were subsequently required to provide services that, far beyond affecting physical change, led to dramatic improvements in the inherent social fabric of the run-down estate and the problems rife within its community.

Determined to avoid the implementation of measures that would allay short-term fears but leave untouched the intrinsic physical layout of the neighbourhood and its susceptibility to anti-social behaviour and deprivation, bptw's options appraisal process involved the execution of an extensive consultative programme on the estate, their readiness to do so incidentally setting the young practice apart from contemporaries who were further removed from direct engagement with potentially confrontational communities. Encouraged by bptw's increasing familiarity around Milton Court and their willingness to listen and respond to local residents, the success of the consultation was a gradual but incremental process which manifest itself in an expanded resident-led steering group for the redevelopment and subsequently a housing management co-operative for a part of the estate. Subsequently, far from a bolt-on activity appeasing the Estate Action Programme's stipulation for working improvements in housing management, tenure diversification and local enterprise, the consultative process genuinely served to reinstate the perception of community cohesion within the local neighbourhood.

After works started on-site in 1993, with residents remaining in occupation throughout, bptw was also one of relatively few practices managing similar projects from an on-site office. While allowing bptw to keep tenants informed throughout the construction process and to discuss any problems arising during the works, the immediacy of the relationship perpetuated by such extensive contact also exacerbated the need for the practice to respond to the more inherent problems facing the Woodpecker Neighbourhood and to demonstrate day-to-day accountability for the work underway.

Central to the redevelopment of the estate, and a direct outcome of the unusually intensive but mutually

beneficial consultative process, bptw's proposals for the regeneration of Milton Court focussed on the return to traditional street architecture and the remedying of the built environment through the recovery of a safe and active communal street frontage and the reconfiguration of the estate to accommodate an increased number of families which would serve to provide an inherently more visible and stable social base for the community.

Required to work within the constraints of the available funding, the need for a cost-effective, ideally cross-subsidising solution and the reluctance for the wholescale demolition of the neighbourhood, bptw subsequently established the case for the radical refurbishment of seven of the blocks, intrinsically involving their demolition and redevelopment from the original slab level, the conversion of 14 maisonettes and the refurbishment of high-rise and low-rise buildings and the 24 storey Hawke Tower; the eighth and only tower block retained, which was chosen to be kept and refurbished since unlike the other seven tower blocks it had recently benefited from the installation of a concierge and thorough security system. Incidentally, the immediate success of the concierge system in Hawke Tower was an unfortunate point of note; there being insufficient funding and widespread concerns about the increased management costs involved in implement this across the remainder of the estate. However, addressing security issues through the physical transformation of the structure and layout of the estate, the redevelopment of the neighbourhood involved the blocking and removal of closed alleys and undercroft areas and their replacement with public spaces, including private and communal gardens and play and parking areas that were safe and overlooked, providing a more open environment for ease of local movement, pedestrian thoroughfare and community interaction.

Structurally, these measures were combined with the redesign of the estate, formerly dominated by tower blocks, to create a less imposing, predominantly low-rise streetscape and communal entrances that opened directly onto the newly landscaped street frontage. Similarly, the entrances on the original low-rise buildings were all reconfigured to create a communal frontage, facing south and west as well as their former east or north only orientation. Addressing the issue of variation in the stairs and lifts in the maisonette blocks, often previously located in concealed corners, bptw's designs led to a reduction

Below and opposite bottom: Sketches produced as part of the initial options appraisal process.
Opposite top: Formerly comprised of tower blocks, the Woodpecker neighbourhood was transformed into a predominantly low-rise streetscape.

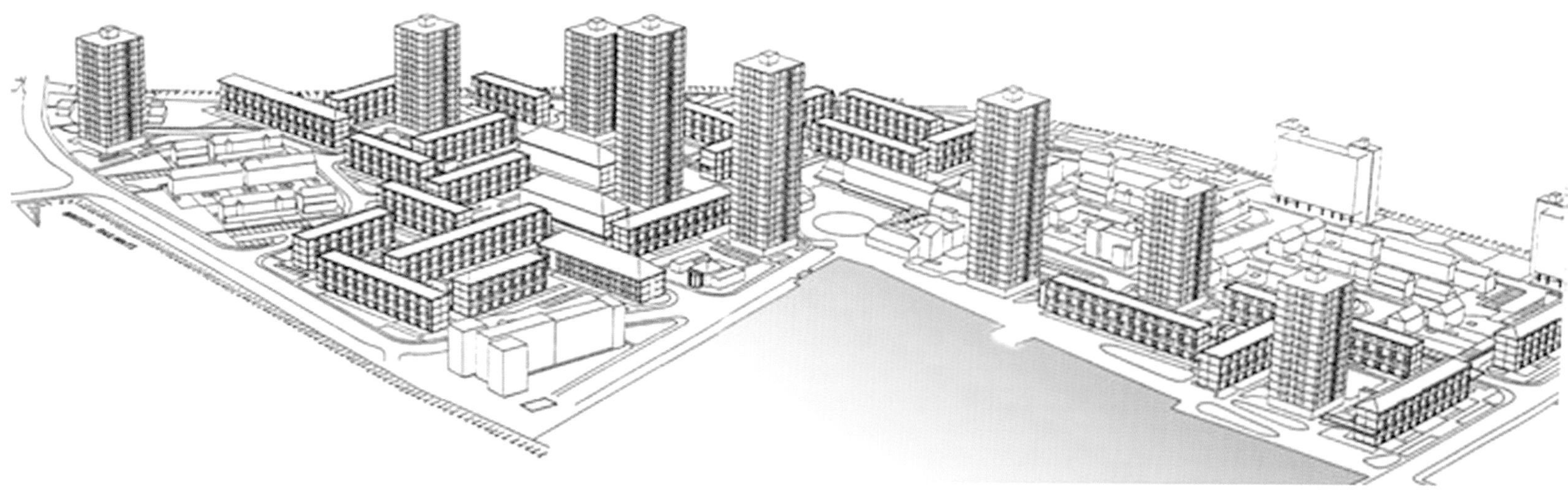

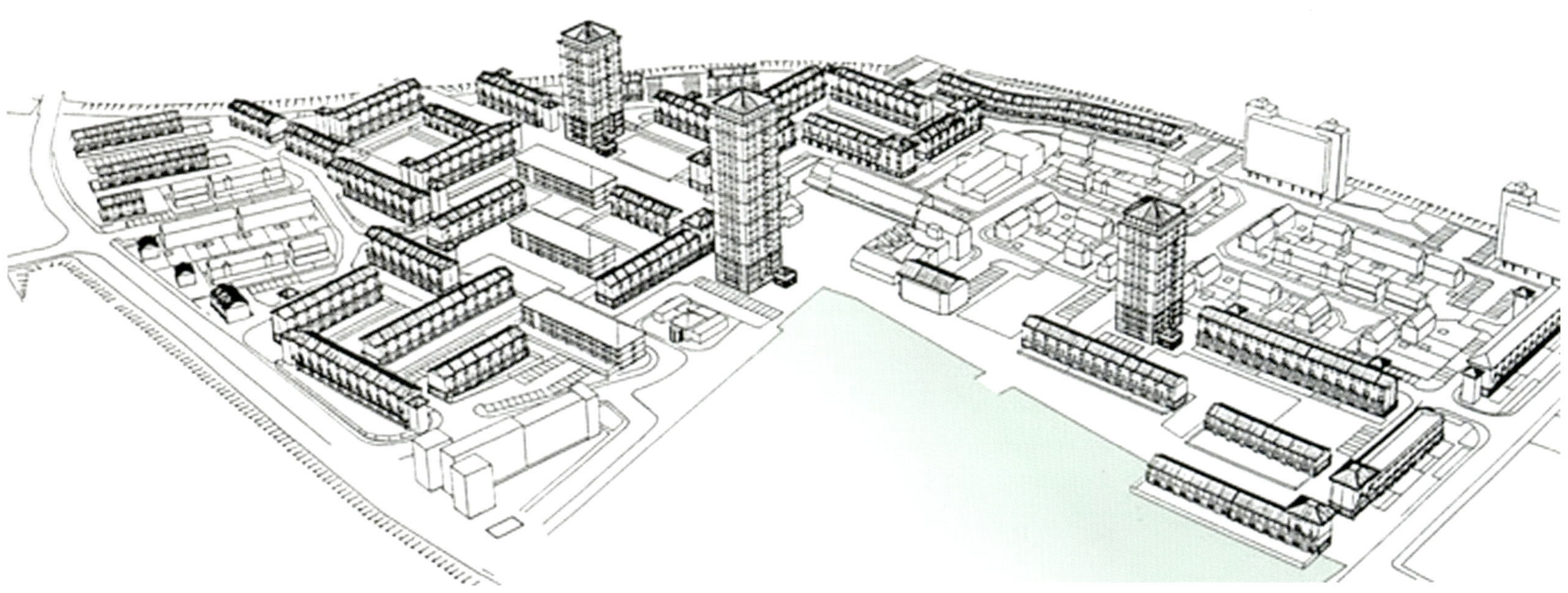

in the height of the buildings and the reversal of their original layout to convert pairs of maisonettes stacked on top of each other into large seven person townhouses.

Improvements to the existing blocks essentially comprised firestopping between dwellings, the elimination of internal mould growth by resolving leaks to external concrete panels, overcladding with insulated render and brickwork and the addition of new pitched roofs. In some cases private balconies were also added, while windows and entrance doors were also replaced throughout. In the process of modernising and refurbishing the internal environment, new kitchens, bathrooms, electrical and plumbing services were refitted throughout all the remaining homes within Milton Court.

Eventually transforming one of the most problematic estates in London, the overall regeneration of Milton Court lasted almost ten years on-site and was delivered through annual rounds of funding issued according to yearly revised cost analysis. Using financial incentives provided through the Estate Action programme, housing management services were added on at estate level with the reintroduction of caretakers and other frontline staff who would instil a new level of community care and a sense of communal responsibility over the physical condition and social management of the estate. As this was only made possible through a physical environment conducive to means of passive surveillance and a community that was sufficiently secure to respond to indirect resident-involvement in the governance of the neighbourhood, this ultimately served to highlight the necessity of good design as an indispensable element of comprehensive estate regeneration, and the Milton Court Masterplan thereby, as a proving ground for the successful implementation of the Estate Action programme.

Opposite: All retained houses were refitted with new kitchens and electrical and plumbing services.
Opposite right: Entrances to the 14 maisonette buildings were reconfigured to create a communal frontage.
Right: The 24 storey Hawke Tower was retained and underwent major internal and external structural refurbishment.

Above: Illustrating the return to traditional street architecture which formed the core of the neighbourhood's redesign.
Opposite: Refurbished blocks showing the new stair towers with lifts, over-cladding and pitched roofs.

Handcroft Road Estate

Directly following their refurbishment work on the St George's & St Patrick's tower blocks in Waltham Forest and the more extensive community regeneration work undertaken on Bishport Avenue in Bristol, bptw were initially selected by the London Borough of Croydon to complete a feasibility study and resident consultation for the regeneration of the Handcroft Road Estate, a 21 block housing estate, built to conventional Radburn principles and accommodating over 360 one and two bedroom properties, in the Greater London Borough of Croydon.

Following the success of this study the practice were subsequently appointed to carry out the full strategic refurbishment of the estate, inclusive of the major structural repairs and the restructuring of many of its fundamental design features. Starting on-site in 1995, the £9 million project was crucially led by feedback from extensive resident consultation which identified, in addition to a common feeling of dissatisfaction in the deteriorating condition, maintenance and management of their housing, a number of pervasive social problems, including graffiti, drug-abuse, and general lack of security, that was negatively impacting upon the lives of the estate's residents. Works were undertaken in four phases by contractors Mansells, Galliford Hodgson, Higgins and Wates

Given the increasing synonymy between these problems and the hard-to-manage lower-level car parks, raised access and play decks, single corridor features and concealed passageways of the Handcroft Road Estate; improvement of the streetscape subsequently became bptw's chief focus for the refurbishment process. Involving the removal of all of the play decks, the blocking of 'no-go' alleyways and corridors and the conversion of every third garage into ground level entrance halls that faced newly well-lit streets, the new design created a more open and transparent communal environment with multiple points of entrance and exit from the buildings that naturally created the opportunity for increased resident interaction, passive surveillance and a heightened sense of security.

In addition to the structural redesign of the estate, bptw also carried out the complete refurbishment of all homes on the estate and made a number of environmental changes to create easily-visible children's play areas and improve the general landscaping, incorporating bollards to regulate car parking negligence, additional planting and seating and increased lighting overall.

Completed over four phases, the final outcome was a success and in conjunction with the efforts of the local authority and partnership between residents, housing

Opposite: Handcroft Road Estate, before refurbishment and regeneration.
Above: Handcroft Road Estate, post-refurbishment.

managers and service providers the estate became a safer, more welcoming environment, supported by an increased sense of ownership from those living on the estate and the service foundations in place to ensure the ongoing social sustainability of the community following the completion of the refurbishment. A reflection of the success of the work carried out and the changed perception of the local environment, Handcroft Road Estate also received a Community Safety Award in 1998.

Opposite and top: Refurbished housing frontages and overlooking improved landscaping and a protected communal area for resident enjoyment.
Bottom: Refurbished balcony area for upper floor maisonettes.

Peckham Partnership

bptw's first multi-award winning scheme and an important precedent in terms of the scale of its delivery, collaborative working and the physical, social and economic change it facilitated; the Peckham Partnership remains one of bptw most defining projects. Exemplifying the strength of consultation-led urban design and the transformational impact of responsible, community-focussed architecture, the seven year project enabled the realisation of bptw's most ambitious ideals for estate regeneration.

Facilitated by a £59.9 million allocation from the inaugural round of Single Regeneration Budget funding in 1995, the Peckham Partnership project was the largest regeneration Challenge Fund project undertaken in Europe at the time. Supplemented by an additional £200 million from a wide range of partners, the scheme involved the masterplanning, consultation and design for the regeneration of over 3,000 homes across five estates in Peckham, South London, contemporaneously the fifth most deprived ward in the UK.

Typifying the inherent physical and socio-economic problems associated with the breakdown of poorly managed and architecturally failing post-war mono-tenured social housing, the five formerly monolithic Peckham estates were reportedly overcome with issues of social decline, deprivation, crime, unemployment and substance misuse; statistically recorded in 1998 as having the highest crime rate across all the London boroughs. Originally a completely flatted high density community comprising over 4,500 local authority managed properties, there was no private investment in housing prior to regeneration of the area. Symptomatic of the general failing of the neighbourhood, there was also a resident turnover of over 30 per cent, resulting in a highly transient community and a self-perpetuating cycle of local instability, unfamiliarity and mistrust; an ideal breeding ground for crime and social disillusionment.

Objectives for the regeneration of the Peckham estates subsequently focussed on addressing the wider issues facing the area. In line with the ethos behind the SRB funding, which had quickly established itself as the key regeneration programme in England, the proposals for Peckham's residential redevelopment were therefore required to incorporate a strong socio-economic programme, providing opportunities for vocational training, educational support and the attraction of new investment including health and transport facilities and local business ventures.

Initiating the overall design and redevelopment process, the London Borough of Southwark's decision to request a masterplan for the five estates was spurred after parts of north Peckham, including the peripheral Gloucester Road area, were seen to have tangibly benefited from earlier Estate Action funding, showing significant social improvement even within the capacity of the relatively limited physical changes. Notably therefore, the local authority's preparatory work for the wider Peckham redevelopment was initially targeted at achieving further Estate Action funding, later switching, to great success, to focus on the partnership working model of the contemporaneously introduced SRB Challenge Fund in 1995.

Responding as part of the successful consortia the London Borough of Southwark's invitation to tender for the regeneration project, bptw worked in collaboration with Pollard Thomas Edwards architects to provide, on the base of overwhelming support from residents and local tenant associations, a winning masterplan for the complete demolition and redevelopment of the five estates. Succeeding against more cautious refurbishment proposals from two alternative consortia, the practice was required to provide evidence of overwhelming tenant support for their perceptibly contentious proposal before their masterplan was eventually implemented.

Opposite left: The Peckham Partnership project, Peckham.
Opposite right: The Peckham estates before redevelopment, illustrating the typically monolithic flat blocks, 'no-go' alleyways and undercroft areas and the formerly inhospitable street frontage.
Above: Elevation showing mixed storey housing blocks (phase five), particularly highlighting the shared entrance ways opening directly onto the main street.

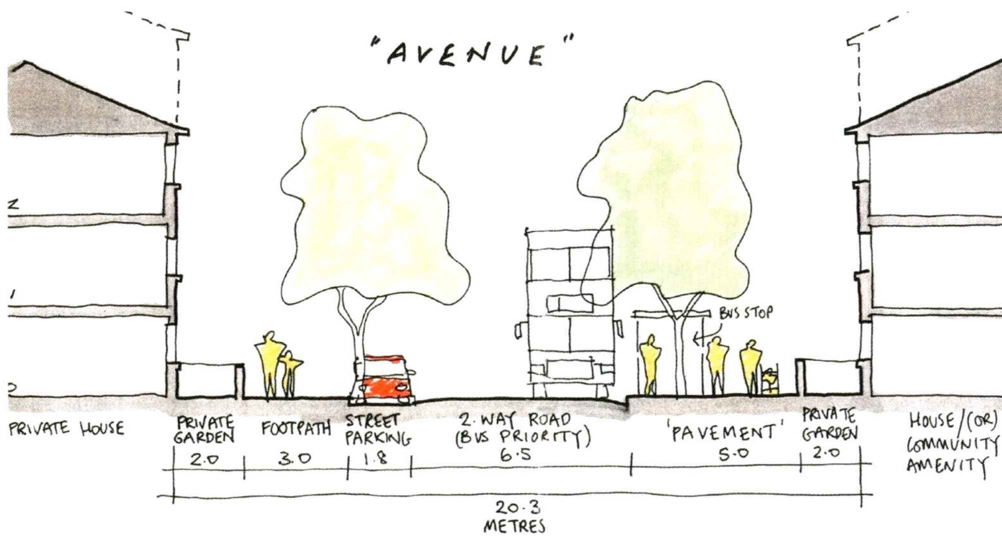

Opposite top: Transforming the former high density, concrete-dominated estate, the Peckham Partnership created an attractive, lower density living environment providing a wide range of low- and medium-rise apartment blocks, mixed-use buildings and larger family houses.
Opposite bottom left: Apartments feature well-sized windows and full-length glazed doors leading to generously proportioned balconies designed to maximise passive surveillance over the public realm.
Opposite bottom right: High detail physical models played a significant role in providing residents with tangible access to the complex masterplan for the five estates.
Left: Professional 3-Dmodel showing the final site layout for the Peckham redevelopment.
Right: Cross section sketch of the proposed central 'avenue', incorporating easily accessible parking space, wide pavements and dimensions that prioritise pedestrian over vehicular movement.

Later working with a range of stakeholders to establish clear objectives for a significant reduction of the density of the estate, the introduction of privately owned property and the collaborative design of over 2,000 high quality new homes, in addition to a meaningful socio-economic programme, a complex and systematic approach to joint-working was quickly implemented. Strong points of action and responsibility for every organisation on the successful design and development team were firmly established, resulting in an effective multi-faceted collaboration between all members of the partnership, in addition to bptw and Pollard Thomas Edwards (PTE) as the main architectural team: contractors Countryside Properties, Laing Partnership Housing, Hyde Housing Association, Family Housing Association, Presentation: Social Investment Agency and SOLFED, a confederation of smaller Housing Associations. Characteristic of any SRB project, the involvement of a wider range of partners throughout the community also included the Lambeth, Lewisham and Southwark Health Authorities, the Metropolitan Police, the Peckham Traders Association and representatives of the residential community, the latter of course being fundamental to the project's overall success.

To this end, bptw set out from the earliest stages to provide the Peckham community with a decisive voice and responsibility over the future of their own public realm. Major public exhibitions generated widespread interest and a huge wave of opinion from residents who had traditionally been given little room for expression. Meanwhile, organised visits to alternative housing developments helped the community develop a more complete understanding of the architects' proposals for the Peckham estates and allowed for the mutual exchange of aspirations for the community.

Further public meetings, model exhibitions, newsletters and group workshops, continued to inform residents of the progress being made with the design and construction process. This specifically allowed for the effective management of the decanting and demolition of the neighbourhood which took place over eight phases; a carefully considered process of maintaining services to existing homes and reducing the amount of disruption to existing residents while ensuring that the new homes functioned well from the outset. Attributable to the inevitable decanting of the lowest-density areas first, this process proved among the most challenging stage of the project; as the highest-density and often most deprived areas became temporarily isolated pockets across the five estates. The resulting increase in degeneration that quickly ensconced the remaining buildings was a stark reminder of the social fragility of the regeneration area, and of the challenges to be overcome through a unified housing management system and the effective placing of mixed-tenure homes. Addressing this, one of the essential considerations of

the masterplan was to dispel the mono-culture of the former flat blocks with the dispersal of mixed-tenure homes in small groups across the area; significantly allowing for the unprecedented introduction of private sale homes in what was formerly the worst part of the area. Tangible rises in local property prices highlighted the contribution this ultimately made to the sustained economic growth of the area. Reconciling this forward thinking approach to development with responsible community focussed social housing, over 60 per cent of the housing stock across the five estates remained under local authority control.

Part of an overall strategy that drew on references from traditional Victorian neighbourhoods, these homes were predominantly designed to comprise of two or three storey houses arranged in terraced rows with private gardens, which were highlighted through the residential consultation process as a particularly attractive feature of the original bptw/PTEa masterplan. Based on similar feedback, the terraces were specifically designed to incorporate features such as sweeping streetscapes, decorative iron-work, gable-fronts and other indicators of conventional 'homeliness' that would establish a sense of belonging and civic pride. Steering away from iconic design, the terraces mirror conventional layout patterns and are arranged along avenues that intersect with main thoroughfares with land-marking corners strengthened by medium-rise apartment blocks, mixed-used buildings and larger family houses.

As well as introducing a more stable social mix into the area, this strategically designed solution was also adopted to provide a greater level of natural surveillance throughout the scheme, augmented in parts by the installation of visible closed circuit television. Further increasing the safety of the neighbourhood, concealed alleyways were designed-out of the five estates, pedestrian thoroughfares were opened up and positioned so as to benefit from improved lighting and public visibility, and a new cycle path was introduced to increase general movement around the Peckham estates.

Above: Smart entranceways and front gardens with shrub planting provide residents a sense of pride and ownership of their properties.
Opposite left: View of phase five, showing the strongly defined corner building and the parking space, allocated in open, landscaped areas overlooked by residential properties.
Opposite right: Site plan of the phased redevelopment of the five estates.

Positioned through the centre of the area formerly occupied by the five estates, the expansive main avenue, overlooked by homes, and lined by wide well-used pavements and easily accessible parking space, was designed to provide a primary route of thoroughfare for tightly-controlled traffic and pedestrian movement through the newly developed area. It also served to directly respond to residents' experience of traversing the former neighbourhood, and the widely shared conviction that it was previously safer for them to walk along the main road around the edges of the estate, instead of on the designated 'yellow-line' secure route through the centre of the area; due to justified concerns over the lack of overlooked space and the predominant misuse of the more isolated sections of the path.

Additionally building on Victorian influences, the masterplan allowed for the introduction of three large new parks which served to add vital open space and green land to the formerly built up area. Serving to lessen the contrast between Peckham estates and the more desirable Camberwell neighbourhood adjacent, the physical and perceived re-organisation of the public realm made a significant difference to the tackling of the wider causes of social and economic decline.

Notably, nearing the completion of the Peckham Partnership regeneration project, in 2001 the London Borough of Southwark dropped to 9th highest place in terms of its crime rate compared to other boroughs across the city; a telling reduction from its previous

position at the top of the list three years earlier, and a direct reflection on the former Peckham estates' new ability to function as an increasingly socially responsible community as opposed to a disparate series of geographically connected residential areas.

The addition of high profile community buildings, including the acclaimed Will Alsop designed Peckham Library and the Peckham Pulse health and leisure facilities, also served to enhance the perception of the previously stigmatised area and created further incentives for future investment in the area. Testifying to the more holistic benefits of the redevelopment process and the SRB funding, over 500 jobs were estimated to have been created as a direct result of the regeneration and, further to the local labour in construction programme operating in the area since 1995, over 1,000 people achieved accredited qualifications in the area.

An appropriate reflection on bptw's developing reputation as an innovative and responsible architectural practice, reconciling traditional community-focussed design with a forward thinking multi-tenured approach, the Peckham Partnership project became bptw's first multi-award winning scheme, achieving short-listing for the ODPM Sustainable Communities Award in 2003, special commendation in the Evening Standards Awards in 2001 and numerous partnering awards over the duration of the regeneration programme.

Opposite top: Replacing former alleys, pedestrian thoroughfares were positioned to benefit from improved lighting and additional features such as strategically placed outdoor seating.
Opposite bottom left: Responding to consultation feedback, designs for the new scheme incorporated private gardens wherever possible, irrespective of housing tenure.
Opposite bottom right: Elevation of low density houses, emphasising the use of conventional terrace features, welcoming colours and adjacent entrances.
Above: Typical view of the conventional Victorian-influenced brick building envelope seen throughout every phase of the Peckham redevelopment.

Studley Community Centre

Completed and officially opened in Spring 2001 by Kate Hoey, then Minister for Sport and MP for the local Stockwell community, Studley Community Centre provided the local neighbourhood with a vibrant, functional and flexible community resource and a means of access to vocational training services, fitness and social activities and the local MP, who would proceed to use the Centre as a future base for her local surgeries.

Part of the overall redevelopment of the Studley neighbourhood which, following the stock transfer of 2,350 properties from the local authority to Hyde Southbank Homes, led to the refurbishment of the neighbourhood as part of a £55 million Estate Renewal Challenge Fund community regeneration programme; bptw were appointed as architects for the £760,000 Community Centre project in 2000 after significantly assisting Hyde Southbank homes with the engagement of local tenants and leaseholders in an extensive consultation process that assisted the overall vote in favour of the stock transfer.

Subsequently building on feedback from this consultation process, bptw provided local residents with the opportunity to fully participate in the design of the Community Centre, which was previously little more than a basic timber construction. Participating in the siting, planning, look, finishing and external works for the proposed building, the newly revitalised Community Centre thereby became a genuine reflection of the Studley community's aspirations; an attractive, modern building with numerous architectural details, inclusive of a striking curved principal facade with full-height timber-detailed glass fronting and a prominent copper roof.

Opposite left: Studley Estate, Peckham.
Opposite right: Exhibition boards used to explain the design process
Above: Studley Community Centre, main facade.

Flexibility of use was a foremost priority, and the finished building is multi-functional in the sense that there are a series of rooms provisionally allocated for different uses including office and meeting space, a crèche area and a function hall; but that each of the activity zones fully interrelate and are linked by a glazed lobby. More than just a corridor or passive entrance area, this space has in turn significantly added to the flexibility of the Community Centre's internal space. Designed to be consciously oversized, the lobby's function has been optimised to accommodate a range of casual uses and activities and, perceived as another active room within the building, the space also accommodates an additional seating area.

Extending the usability of the internal environment, the rear garden is also fully adaptable for use as a crèche, or general community function area.

The centre was also designed and orientated to take maximum advantage of natural daylight and ventilation without excessive solar gain. Sustainable materials were used wherever possible for the construction and finishes and the design incorporates reclaimed flooring in addition to recycled wood fibre blown cellulose insulation throughout the Centre.

Effectively managed by residents, the Studley Community Centre remains a popular and well-used community resource, its intensive use testifying to the need for architects to prioritise the functionality of their designs to provide responsible buildings that crucially, can be adapted by the end users to meet the requirements of the local community, while also serving as an aesthetically appealing component of the local streetscape.

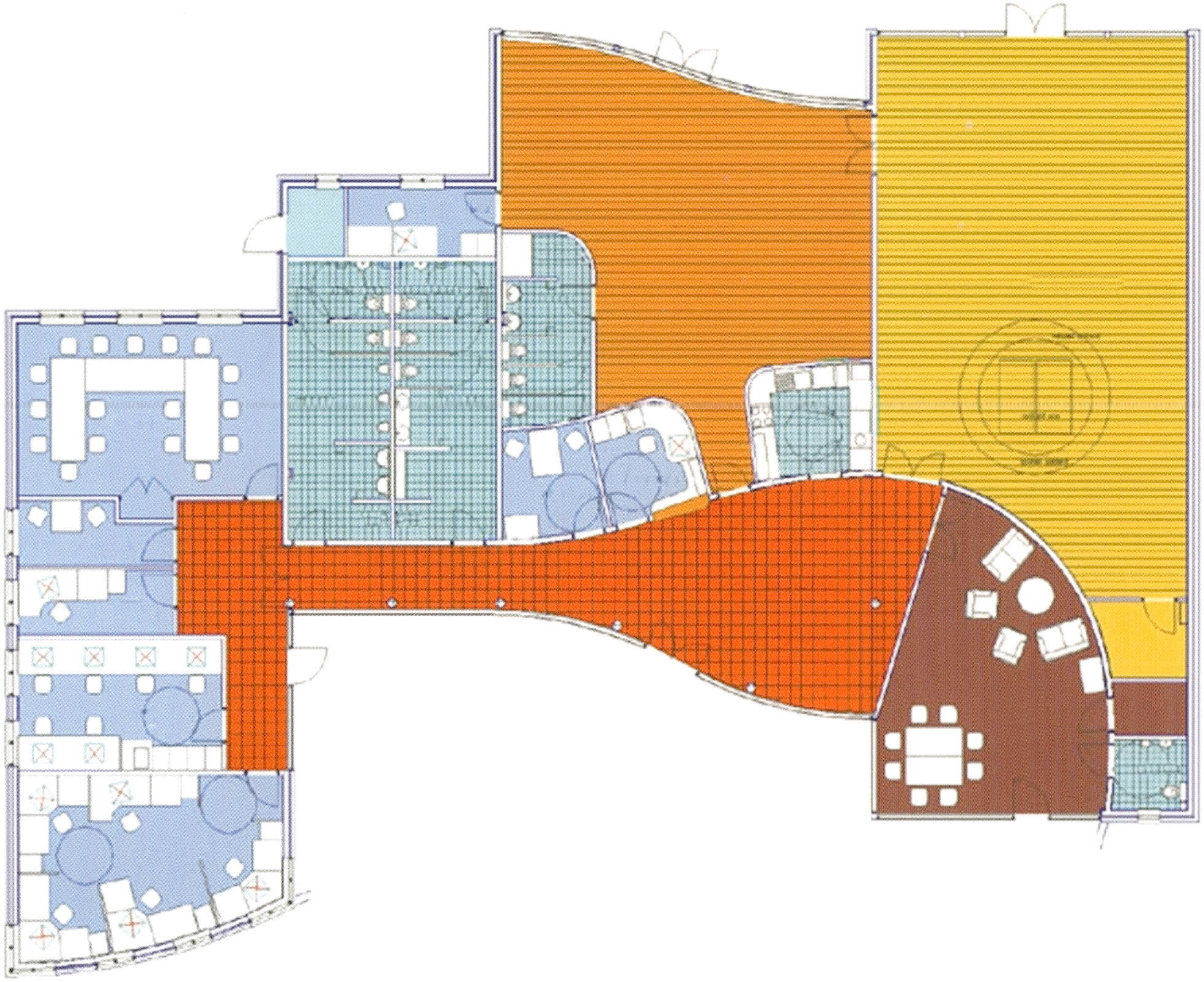

Opposite top: Use of the multi-purpose function hall for as a community fitness facility.
Opposite bottom: Community Centre plan, illustrating its expansive public frontage, exaggerated lobby area and the variation in the size and capacity of the internal rooms.
Above: The crèche's interior features striking colours and bold lighting to mirror the building's external design, it is also fluidly linked with the centre's other rooms.

Lime Tree House

Serving as bptw partnership's first elderly person's residential project, Lime Tree House was completed in October 2000 as an additional, off-site development forming part of the overall regeneration of the five Peckham Partnership estates.

Located on the site of former local authority owned post-war prefabricated buildings; space for the scheme became available as a result of decanting into surrounding regeneration schemes and the transfer to new homes. Lime Tree House provides independent accommodation for older people within a Category 2.5 sheltered environment offering the support required to house people with varying degrees of mobility and needs for a diverse range of care packages.

Selected in 1998 by Hyde Housing in partnership with the London Borough of Southwark, bptw partnership was initially appointed for the £3 million contract to provide 37 self-contained flats and communal facilities for the development. Built by contractor John Laing Partnership, the design focussed on the provision of

Opposite left: Lime Tree House, Peckham. *Opposite right*: Layout plan for Lime Tree House showing the later extension. *Above*: Sketch illustrating how the layout of Lime Tree House creates a protected and enclosed private realm for residents while maintaining strong links with the surrounding public realm.

Top: Lime Tree House, 2001, view highlighting sensitive landscaping and easily navigable garden layout.
Bottom: View of the internal recreation area.
Opposite: View of Lime Tree house from the north.

a safe and supportive community environment, enhancing social engagement and the connection between the facility's internal space and the outside community, while addressing the need to provide a co-existing sense of community and independent living for the elderly residents of the sheltered care environment.

Each flat has been designed to generous Lifetime Homes space standards and has adaptable shower rooms and kitchenettes. Large picture windows, to floor level, enhance the spaciousness and natural light entering each flat. While all areas of the scheme are wheelchair accessible, seven apartments have been designed specifically for wheelchair occupancy, five of which have direct access to the gardens.

Similarly reinforcing the interaction between the internal and external environment, bptw designed a south-facing communal garden room, similar in concept to a conservatory, which became a focal point for the residents of Lime Tree House. Incorporating large sliding screens and views of an extensively landscaped garden, the design purposely aimed to provide an incentive for residents to engage with the outside natural environment and to prevent any sense of containment inside the facility. Similarly, drawing on social approaches to architecture in The Netherlands and the notion of 'living streets', the design for Lime Tree House aimed to reduce as far as possible a reliance on corridors to create usable spaces that optimise natural light and provide areas for meeting, interacting and activity.

Further reinforcing the openness, homeliness and non-institutional appeal of Lime Tree House, bptw focussed on using form, materials, colour and lighting to augment its contemporary, non-uniform approach to the care facility.

High quality materials such as copper wrapping around the underside of the roof detail and fringing the ceiling-to-floor glazed doors and window panels have been applied to the building, whilst internally, timber panels

wrap around the walls into the main space of the facility. Traditional construction methods and robust materials such as red brick were utilised to ensure a thermally efficient, economically sustainable and cost-effective solution was achievable. Natural materials such as iroko and ash were used in key locations, emphasising features such as the entrance canopy, reception counter, window seats and conservatory.

Testament to the success of the initial scheme, bptw were appointed in 2004 to carry out a second phase of development on Lime Tree House, to a contract value of £2 million. Having initially designed the building with the potential for later expansion of the facility in mind and, following feedback from residents and staff at the home, the extension subsequently adopted a similar design concept to the existing building, providing an additional 17 flats along with further computing space, offices and a staff room.

Notably, beyond the provision of a safe and supportive residential environment, careful management of Lime Tree House has also allowed the development to provide a resource for the wider community. Making best use of the communal facilities, the building also includes a residents' laundry, clinic and hairdressing room which, along with a regular programme of events, including jumble sales and musical performances, help maximise the interaction between residents, staff and outside users.

Opposite: Front and rear elevations from the early stages of the design process.
Left: Purposely designed as a suitable connecting point for the future expansion of the building, the extension to Lime Tree House would later be constructed alongside the three storey stairwell.
Right: The extension, opened in Autumn 2007, draws on the shape of the design and the colours used throughout the original building.
Overleaf: Lime Tree House, Spring 2008.

Charlton Triangle

An exemplary model of successful stock transfer and the effective joint-working of btpw and local housing association partnerships, the £35 million Charlton Triangle scheme was also, incidentally, the practice's first major project in Greenwich. Involving the stock transfer and regeneration of 1,286 homes across four estates and a tower block in the Charlton area under the Estate Renewal Challenge Fund, bptw were involved from the outset, fundamentally assisting in the consultation and management process which led to the initial stock transfer from local authority control.

Originally enlisted by Family Housing Association in 1999, bptw were engaged to convey to the residents of the Charlton Triangle, the benefits of the proposals for the transfer in control of their council-owned homes to the newly established Charlton Triangle Homes Housing Association, a subsidiary of Family Housing Association; individually reputable and experienced in community consultation, Family and bptw formed an effective and influential community regeneration team. In advance of the stock transfer ballot each home was visited a minimum of three times and the opinions of local residents were collated to form the base of the housing association's proposals for the future redevelopment of the area.

Empowered by their visible contribution to the decisions affecting the shape of their community, residents came out in strong favour of the transfer, and further to the

success of the ballot, bptw were subsequently appointed to provide the design and cost consultation for the internal refurbishment and refitting of over 900 homes, including the redevelopment of external landscaping and the installation of play areas and secured entrances for the blocks. The wider redevelopment of the Charlton Triangle also included a design solution for Coutts House, an 11 storey flat block which would be demolished and replaced by high quality terraced houses and medium-rise apartment blocks, and later, the incorporation of four new-build schemes that would begin on-site in 2006.

Following the successful stock transfer, tenant liaison officers were introduced to help co-ordinate the regeneration process and to ensure residents remained central to the key decisions being made for their community; a variety of methods were subsequently employed to engage as wide a range of residents as possible, including the creation of steering committees, one-to-one consultations and a number of residents' groups concentrating on the more holistic development of education, employment and diversity within the community, as well as retaining community interest in the future maintenance of the neighbourhood, as the properties remained occupied throughout the extensive and time-consuming refurbishment process, it was a particularly important means of keeping residents informed throughout the various stages of work, reducing the impact of the disruption and ensuring full resident co-operation.

Opposite: Charlton Triangle, London Borough of Greenwich.
Above: Involving over 900 homes, the internal repair and refurbishment programme affected every home across the Charlton Triangle.

In close collaboration with contractors Higgins and Galliford Hodgson who worked concurrently on different parts of the site, bptw subsequently carried out an extensive repair and refurbishment programme that affected every building across the Charlton Triangle and included the redesigning of kitchens, bathrooms, windows and entrances, in addition to extensive structural repair work, rewiring and a refit of heating and ventilation systems on a total of more than 900 homes.

An extensive, costly and challenging process, meeting the Estate Renewal Challenge Funds objectives for the redevelopment of Charlton Triangle required a careful financial and technical balancing act over the course of the project. For instance, early on in the process ambitious targets for the simultaneous refurbishment of properties needed revision as unanticipated levels of necessary services work left too many homes being worked on for an extended period of time. Requiring similar reorganisation of construction time and contingency funding, fundamental problems inherent in the existing housing stock led to an increase of necessary repairs expenditure for the project; a problem characteristic of the reliance of Estate Renewal Challenge Fund schemes' on the pre-transfer condition of housing stock.

Similar complications surrounding the physical condition and financial viability of working with original buildings surrounded the redevelopment of Coutts House, an 11

Top left: Demolition of the 11 storey Coutts House.
Top right: An integral part of the public consultation, physical models played a large role in making the design process accessible for the local community.
Bottom: Coutts House before demolition.
Opposite: Blocks refurbished as part of the Charlton Triangle project.

storey housing block on a contaminated, former quarry site on Charlton Church Lane. Restricted to building off the original foundations and in the context of the Victorian and Edwardian houses opposite the former housing block, bptw designs eventually transformed a heavily contaminated, steeply sloping site into a new residential scheme comprising 36 new houses and apartments for affordable rent.

Arranged in a long terrace, punctuated with a series of three storey pavilions and book-ended by medium-rise flat blocks at either end, the homes feature brick, render and timber panelled cladding, pitched roofs and boldly coloured secure entrances, giving the scheme a significant local identity. Remaining responsive to the constraints of the site and budget, the arrangement of the building maximises the gradient of the site to provide residents with striking views over the city.

Reconciling the need to provide cost-effective design solutions and high quality refurbishment improvements in light of these challenges, bptw's cost consultancy team came into its own, proving through effective internal collaboration, how the practice's multi-disciplinary approach heightened its ability to effectively manage projects through all stages of planning and construction. The Charlton Triangle project also afforded a valuable lesson in drawing the line between the economic viability of refurbishment as opposed to demolition and new build; following detailed options appraisals suggesting that

certain parts of Charlton Triangle were more efficiently dealt with via the latter, approval for the last phase of the project was finally achieved in 2006.

Consisting of four new build developments in Victoria Way, Rectory Field Crescent, Bramhope Lane and East Mascalls, this will result in 225 homes of mixed-tenure for affordable rent and private sale, including houses and apartments. Featuring brick, render and timber cladding, the homes are contemporary in design and provide spacious living areas and private amenity.

Opposite: Official opening of Charlton Church Lane, 16 July 2006, formerly Coutts House.
Above: Rear view along a refurbished block. Mirroring houses were separated by newly landscaped grass verges and generous footpaths, removed from vehicular access routes.

Kender

Reinforcing bptw partnership's reputation as community regeneration specialists, bptw were appointed in 2000 by the London Borough of Lewisham to develop the masterplan for the redevelopment of over 1,300 homes on the Kender Triangle neighbourhood in New Cross, South London. Accounting for the refurbishment of over 720 homes and the implementation of a range of structural repairs including the refitting and modernisation of kitchens and bathrooms across the scheme, the masterplan also incorporated the development of approximately 500 affordable new build homes.

Responding to feedback from community consultation, proposals for the redevelopment of the Kender neighbourhood were significantly influenced by the local residents' concerns over the security of the public realm, the lack of safe, well-lit thoroughfares across the estate and the limited permeability of the neighbourhood, leading to a perceived sense of confinement among residents.

Directly impacting on the re-organisation of the Kender Estate's external space, the residents' concerns over perceptibly stigmatised housing blocks and the lack of general physical or social cohesion within the Kender Triangle were addressed by the masterplan in the proposed elimination of undercroft areas which were replaced by private gardens, and the creation of traditional street patterns with an active frontage and mirroring 'fronts and backs', to provide increased opportunity for community interaction, passive surveillance and a heightened sense of security in the public realm. The reorganisation of the public

Left: Kender Triangle neighbourhood, New Cross.
Opposite top: Typical Kender Triangle housing block, before refurbishment.
Opposite bottom: The White House, post-refurbishment.

realm to allow for increased green space in the form of community parks and play areas, in addition to the creation of a new road, footpaths and cycle routes designed through the centre of the Triangle also had a significant impact on passage through the estate, significantly allowing for a greater sense of interactivity with the surrounding communities.

With residents remaining in occupation as the redevelopment was underway, a thorough ongoing consultation process enabled the community to remain fully engaged with the ongoing refurbishment, ensuring satisfaction in the final result and greater co-operation while the work was being carried out. Residents also contributed to the physical re-design of the external and internal environments of their newly refurbished homes and to the most integral features of the wider regeneration, including the selection of colours for the new aluminium cladding of Hatfield Close Tower Blocks, which had been visually enhanced within bptw's masterplan to reflect their prominent location at the Gateway to the Borough.

Allocated funding from the local authority's direct expenditure, the practice was subsequently contracted to complete phase one of the redevelopment programme which involved the refurbishment of the White House containing specialised frail elderly accommodation, two 12 storey residential tower blocks at Hatfield Close, and the detailed design and implementation of the refurbishment of an additional 355 existing homes, predominantly featuring medium density, low-rise housing.

Requiring particular sensitivity to residents' needs, from both the design team and Botes Building as contractor, the refurbishment of the White House was also carried out with residents in occupation, requiring considerable care in managing the project and ordering the sequence of works to allow for a rolling decant programme within the building itself.

Consisting of 48 one bedroom self-contained flats and communal facilities within a previously monolithic seven storey building, the £2.9 million refurbishment of the White House, completed in 2002, was the spearhead for the overall refurbishment bptw were undertaking on behalf of the London Borough of Lewisham.

Fulfilling the objective to improve the White House through the refitting of bathrooms and kitchens in every flat, thereby bringing the outdated housing stock in line with current ambulant disabled standards, the refurbishment also required the complete replacement of mechanical and electrical services and a general enhancement of the White House's external wall using internal thermal lining, overcladding and the installation of improved double glazing.

Responding to the lack of natural light to internal spaces and good quality shared meeting space for residents within the White House, the refurbishment of the building also included the creation of a garden room, inspired by the success of bptw's earlier work on Lime Tree House in Peckham. Accounting for the varying degrees of mobility and the high proportion of those confined to the internal environment, the communal glass-fronted garden room was positioned to look out into the centre of a newly created landscaped garden and crucially provided a space that offered residents the opportunity

Opposite top: Hatfield Close, exterior. Wrapped in a lightweight aluminium rainscreen system, off-set with contrasting brick work at ground floor level.
Opposite bottom: Multi-functional community room, designed to provide a spacious, airy and naturally well-lit interior environment.
Above: External water feature, designed to form a striking connection with the proportions, shape and colour of the facade of the White House.

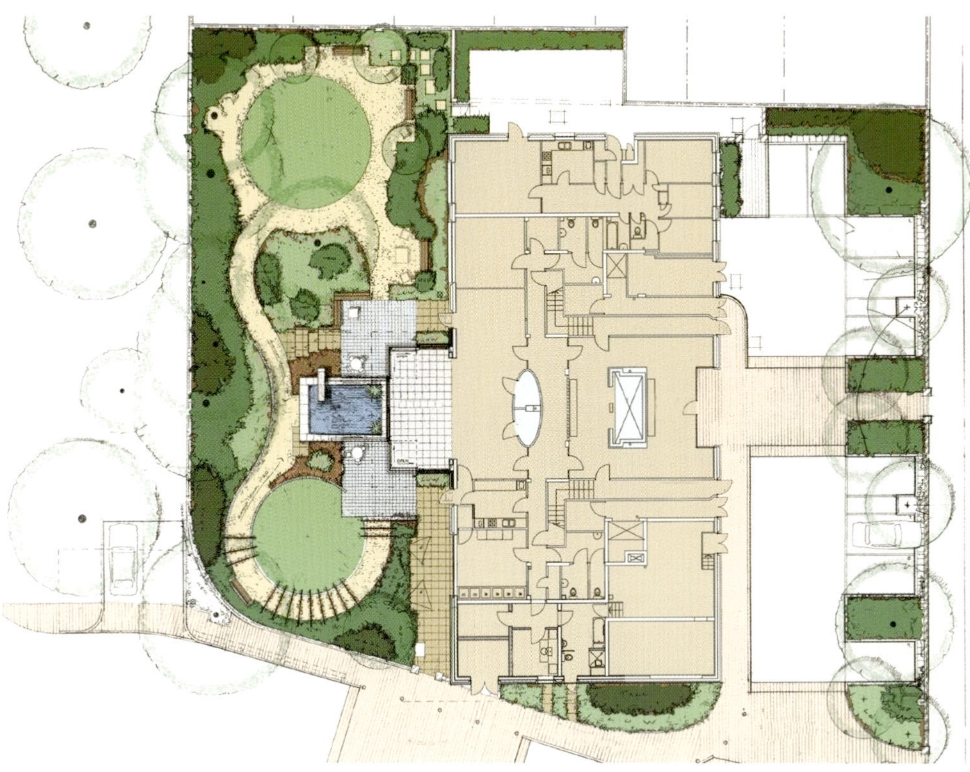

for social interaction, light and warmth while making the most of the White House's radically improved external appearance. The further introduction of a ground floor hairdressing room and facilities for internet access also made a significant contribution to the sense of community among the residents.

Completing the refurbishment and landscaping process, the white mosaic tiles of the White House's former exterior were replaced with a modern insulated terracotta rainscreen cladding system and aluminium double glazed windows that create a distinct identity for the building with a discernibly contemporary and non-institutional appeal.

Particularly befitting the cost-effective and efficient delivery of the White House and exemplifying the strength of the relationship between bptw's internal disciplines, the practice's architectural and cost consultancy teams worked in close partnership with each other, and the London Borough of Lewisham, throughout the duration of the scheme which in total cost £35 million for the refurbishment aspect.

Notably, while the careful financial organisation allowed for the most appropriate and timely refurbishment to be carried out under strict funding criteria; the success of the project continues to evolve and develop in accordance with the ongoing New Cross Gate New Deal for Communities (NDC), a ten year programme supporting the sustainable regeneration of the area. Exemplifying this, the ongoing framework for development has built on the original masterplan with proposals for the addition of the NDC Healthy Living Centre; a significant development project providing a significant architectural and social focal point and serving as a catalyst for the further regeneration of the Kender Estate and the whole of the New Cross Gate Community.

Opposite: Ground floor plan of The White House, illustrating the multi-purpose internal communal rooms and carefully designed garden layout.
Above: Hatfield Close highlighting the new aluminium cladding.
Bottom: Community room looking onto the water feature at The White House.

Raising Expectations

Despite the success of bptw's work and their considerable growth in terms of staff, expertise and reputation within the housing sector, as the millennium arrived, the practice was still, self-acknowledgely, a relatively minor player among their architectural contemporaries.

Accordingly, even foresight would allow for reasonable surprise when, five years later, from a supposed outsiders place on the shortlist, bptw partnership was announced 'Architectural Practice of the Year' at *Building Magazine*'s annual awards ceremony. Secured in the face of considerable competition from several larger, more high profile practices the accolade was received as a welcome tribute to the practice's dedication to quality service and responsible community design. Significantly, it was also testament to the success of bptw's enlightened approach to its staff and a reflection of the unique way in which the practice's founding vision had manifest itself within overall business practice.

In addition to gaining *Building*'s attention, bptw's listing in the *Sunday Times 100 Best Companies to Work For (SMEs)* since the start of the award in 2004, also underlined their commitment to placing people, staff alongside the communities they worked for, at the centre of the practice's business policy; and the level of internal engagement and loyalty the practice received from their employees in return.

Continuing to the present day to feature in the Best Companies List, bptw partnership is now annually assessed, by its own employees, for the quality of its leadership, internal relationships, personal growth, fair dealing over pay and benefits and record for giving something back to society. However, not consciously allied to the practice's corporate objective, the *Best Company* label remains more a symbol of bptw's organic growth as a business organisation; its earliest foundations resting in the achievement of quality assurance in 1994, eventually progressing to the employee-led presentation for Investors in People re-accreditation in 2005.

Belying the ease with which bptw staff adopted their key role in the management of the practice, the process of achieving this extended over a five year period of complex internal development; spurred by the announcement that founding partner Roger Taylor would be stepping down in 2002 after a career spanning 15 years with bptw, and that Anna Parkinson, David Welsh and Robert Silcock would subsequently be appointed as new partners in the practice. While allowing for the responsibility of a broader range of client relations, an increased project workflow and the significant rise in junior staff among the then 45 strong practice, the extended management tier also underlined the need to formalise the strategic direction of the practice under the eyes of the continuing partners, and the necessity of ensuring their buying into the practice's ideals and business ambition.

Hence, the first structured business planning review was established. Taken out of the office for a day of reflection and discussion on the future of the practice, the partners collectively drafted bptw's first business plan; a simple but unanimously supported vision of the practice's aims and

View of the completed CABE award-winning Elmington redevelopment, 2005.

values. Considerably more aspiration-driven than financially-directed, its unique selling point, particularly within the contemporaneous architectural sector, was notably its concentration on people and the staff development strategy at its hub.

However, while incorporating an improvement in the direction of internal communication, personal performance appraisals, annual staff and client satisfaction surveys and increasingly more structured training programmes, the business plan essentially reinforced the basic cultural ethos bptw had always upheld. Nevertheless, serving as an official framework on which they were able to demonstrate their realisation of professional objectives through the effective management and development of their staff, it also enabled the practice to receive their first Investors in People accreditation in 2002.

Three years later, the second business plan was a reflection of considerably more significant progress. Developed by the associates working with the partners, the comprehensive document was the outcome of a detailed review of practice management processes and the work of six, newly formed, business planning teams comprising of members of staff who elected to join throughout the year. Uptake of this policy meant 85 per cent of bptw staff were actively engaged in business planning activities by 2005 and the same year, epitomising the centrality of the employees' involvement and engagement with practice ideals, the re-accreditation of the Investors in People award was achieved through a staff-led presentation. Noted as unique by the Investors in People assessor, it was a welcome demonstration that the partners' vision held firm across each strata of the practice.

While enforcing best practice internally, the business planning teams also had a significant part to play in the introduction of the organisation's social calendar and a schedule of external events for staff recreation. Comprising of sports tournaments, annual picnics open to friends and family, designated monthly social evenings and the time-honoured 'away-day' where staff collectively spent a day out of the office in an alternative UK or European destination; the events quickly developed into tradition and still remain a defining element of the practice's family-focussed approach to inclusiveness, staff welfare and reasonable working hours.

Given that the practice was dealing with almost 100 projects a year by the close of 2005, the effort of maintaining this equilibrium was a careful balancing act. From the turn of the millennium, housing had become an increasingly high priority on the UK political and social agenda and the associated raft of government policies, ambitious political targets and newly introduced funding streams had a considerable impact upon the volume and shape of bptw's work.

Similarly, as climate change became an exponentially more prominent political, economic and social concern, the issue of environmental sustainability in the housing sector also garnered increased column inches; with notable effect on design, construction and marketing within the same arena.

Launched at the turn of the century, the Millennium Commission's £2 billion investment in National Lottery projects was the first in a series of much lauded funding initiatives that would characterise the drive for change and new growth over the next five years. It was also among those with the least impact on bptw who secured little in the way of direct funding from the scheme, benefiting more from the relative lack of crowding in the social housing market as significant numbers of heir architectural rivals pursued funded projects elsewhere.

Shortly afterwards however, July 2000 saw the arrival of one of the new centuries most defining policies. Led by Deputy Prime Minister John Prescott and entitled 'Quality and Choice: A Decent Home for All', the green paper publication heralded the Labour government's public service target to ensure all social housing would meet set standards of decency by 2010.

Adopted at a time when 42 per cent of social housing stock was deemed short of the 'Decent Home' standard, the paper identified a £19 billion backlog of repairs and modernisation work for the 1.2 million local authority owned homes alone.

Crucial to the perpetuation of bptw's work in stock transfer consultations and the delivery of large scale refurbishment and renewal schemes, the paper incongruously followed on the back of the Estate Renewal Challenge Fund to pigeonhole the devolution of housing stock as the primary means of securing investment for the necessary repair work; via delegation to Arms Length Management Organisations, participation in Private Finance Initiative schemes or transfer to one or more housing associations. However, while the Decent Homes standard, later reinforced by Prescott's 2003 *Decent Homes Target Implementation Plan* and the *Sustainable Communities* action programme, was debatably a more strategic approach to housing and regeneration, it was unquestionably one that impacted upon the focus of bptw's engagement with its clients.

The economics of providing homes to meet the stringent new targets, on time and to budget, required the practice to become more involved with private sector developers and invariably with larger, design-centred projects with higher-densities, mixed tenures and opportunities for cross-subsidising. Often leading to the inclusion of a range of housing types within individual design schemes, and integrating mixed-use facilities for the purpose of community welfare, education and commerce, bptw was also required to significantly review its own strategies towards the breakdown of mono-tenured and socially segregated housing.

Opposite left: Visualisation of houses at Lymington Fields, Barking.
Opposite right: The Laurels Healthy Living Centre & Turners Court, Tottenham.

Refining their design and consultation process accordingly, bptw's work on the Laurels Healthy Living Centre, their first major mixed-use scheme consisting of 71 new affordable homes and the provision of much needed NHS Primary Care Trust services in Tottenham North London, highlighted the practice's ability to adapt to these changes. Building on the same fundamental notion of care, major consultation was undertaken with the care provider and local authority regarding the requirements for the health facilities, while the opinions of the neighbouring residents were sought towards the housing element. Generating means of overcoming the inevitable difficulty of first-hand community consultation in new build developments, bptw also used the project to introduce a feedback system whereby the residents' evaluation of the development was collated and could be fed into future new-build programmes.

Opportunely, bptw's invitation to bid in a consortia with Countryside Properties and a group of Housing Associations for the 2003 London Wide Initiative (LWI), would allow the practice's commitment to new design solutions to come to the fore. Characterising the emergence of regionally specific development agencies, the government backed initiative was founded on English Partnership's purchase of 15 development sites across Inner and Greater London and the projected delivery of up to 5,000 new homes, 1,500 of which were to be made available for key workers under shared-equity plans.

The successful bid resulted in appointment on three sites. Hunters & Partners took the lead design role on the development of the former Catford Stadium site in the London Borough of Lewisham while bptw partnership assumed responsibility for the London Road site in Croydon and were jointly appointed with Watkins Gray International for the development of Lymington Fields for Presentation SIA in the London Borough of Barking and Dagenham. Both were projects of considerable size and complexity and after lengthy negotiations planning approval for the masterplan for Lymington Fields was to be achieved in early 2008; a testament to the tenacity and pragmatism of the architects' joint-working partnership.

Notably, as procurement processes increasingly afforded contractors and developers the lead role in managing project design schemes, bptw's reputation as a reliable and responsible collaborative partner began to benefit the future of the practice as much as its ever-more commended quality design and architectural innovation.

The practice's strategic decision to open a new office in Epping in 2002 firmly reinforced their standing in this arena. Incorporating bptw partnership's consultative focus and internal working structure where, despite the increasing number of staff, partners still played a leading hands-on role in each project; the new office comprised of, and remains to the current day, a relatively small, widely respected, partner and associate-led technical team. It was a decision, and a subsequent new pool of staff, that would lend valuable support to the practice's reputation as an attentive, sympathetic and efficient collaborator.

Having crucially proven their respect for the mutual demands placed on contractors and developers and an ability to understand the economic and time-scale pressures of the delivery process, bptw subsequently began to gain appointments with other lead designers, including the implementation of a number of high profile projects, ranging from the high density development

Top: View of the highly acclaimed Donnybrook Quarter.
Bottom: Catherine Grove; a conversion combining contemporary style with sympathetic restoration and reinstatement of the former Victorian school's original features.
Opposite: Luxury 'loft-style' apartments have been created, incorporating mezzanine sleeping galleries which take advantage of the scale of the original classroom windows and double-height spaces.
Overleaf: The new Axis development of 24 contemporary homes stands on the former site of the Maze Hill School in Greenwich.

Apartments
Axis

Top: Polychrome Court, Waterloo.
Bottom: Garden view at 'The Spire' development at Tushmore Roundabout, Crawley.

at Lough Road for Countryside and the innovative Donnybrook Quarter in Bow with Willmott Dixon. Both projects; respectively developed for Newlon and Circle Anglia Housing Associations, received widespread acclaim.

bptw's growing reputation also led to their appointment on a range of high specification developments in the private residential market; an opportunity that would allow the practice to explore its approach to light and internal space with slightly less stringent financial constraints than their usual projects entailed. In 2001 the practice was responsible for the conversion of a former Victorian School Building in Catherine Grove where bptw were appointed by Durkan New Homes to create luxury loft-style apartments from the internal reconfiguration and sympathetic external restoration of the building's features and later, the Axis development, consisting of 24 new apartments and mews houses adjacent to the Royal Park in Greenwich. Similar work for Higgins Homes also included the development of Copper Point, a contemporary inner-city development of luxury town houses and apartments overlooking Southwark Park in Rotherhithe, and Polychrome Court, a development of 12 inner city homes, designed to be car-free, in close proximity to London Waterloo Station. Each of these projects provided bptw with invaluable experience of the private market and a new base of experience for incorporation in future mixed-tenure schemes.

However, as delivery targets continued to flood the affordable housing sector, along with increased pressure to simultaneously accommodate improved methods of construction and a reduction in carbon emissions, private residential work remained firmly secondary in the practice's priorities. The practice's attention instead turned to the 2002 Housing Corporation's Challenge Fund which ring-fenced money from the Approved Development Programme, for Housing Association-led bidders to deliver new homes quickly and cost-effectively.

Concurrent with the launch of the London Wide Initiative, the government also invited bids for Challenge Fund II and this led to bptw being invited to join a consortia led by Genesis Housing Group. The consortia would become Gentect Homes; a virtual alliance company established along with contractors Allenbuild Ltd, The Durkan Group, Hill Partnerships, McCann Homes and fellow architectural practice SHP. The bid put together was not only successful but secured the largest portion of the Challenge Fund II programme, providing a major contribution to Genesis Housing's development programme and vision. The consortia developed into a legal entity in April 2005 and was soon-after re-launched under the name of Logic Homes in 2006 after securing a Housing Corporation partner status grant. The shareholding partners became involved in every aspect of the business operation, which, in conjunction with the Housing Corporations' objectives, continues to focus on the provision of new mixed-tenure homes including affordable rented properties and houses for shared ownership options.

Exemplifying this, bptw were appointed to work as lead architects on some of the consortia's most pioneering projects including the Peglar Way and Tushmore Roundabout sites in Crawley, collectively providing a combination of 56 flats and family homes for key workers, and Cranes Farm Road, a development of 48 low-rise homes and 12 flats for affordable rent and shared ownership within a tenure 'blind' scheme in Basildon in the Thames Gateway, where the rented and part-owned homes are indistinguishable from each other in terms of construction material and location within the site.

Opposite: View of completed Copper Point, high quality, contemporary apartments and town houses overlooking Southwark Park and featuring attractive external finishes, including copper cladding and cedar panelling.
Above: View of Tramway House in Erith post completion. Designed using off-site construction principles. Volumetric units and steel frames have been used for the first phase of the development. The second phase was built with innovative piling systems, light-weight steel frames and volumetric units. The building wraps around an enclosed south-facing and landscaped courtyard area.
Right: View of volumetric units.

Including timber frame solutions and prefabricated bathroom 'pods' that were able to be constructed off-site, each of the three projects incorporated the latest innovations in modern methods of construction into their building process; a key feature of Logic Homes' ready-made supply chain that was integral to its capacity to provide affordable, high quality housing to tight time frames.

Notably, in the exploration of affordable housing options and new means of driving efficiency in delivery, bptw had already used various modern methods of construction on a number of projects. Appointments from the Orbit Group to design Tramway House in Erith and Tower Hamlets Community Housing for the development of Siege House in Wapping both utilising volumetric construction solutions, with a second phase at Tramway House using light gauge steel frame.

Notably however, as the range of mixed-use and mixed-tenure schemes became increasingly more prevalent within the practice's portfolio, so did the complexities of the modern methods of construction systems, which were seen by private developers as less flexible for the nature of decision making on private sale housing.

Nevertheless, encouraged by Housing Corporation funding requirements, the concept of this technology continued to dominate working framework requirements with developers and housing associations, including Logic Homes, reflecting the collective desire to bring together modern methods of construction, effective design and strong supply-chain cost-efficiency.

The culmination of this debate was the 2005 Design for Manufacture, or '£60k House', competition, managed by English Partnerships, on behalf of John Prescott, Deputy Prime Minister, challenged the construction and design industry to construct a home for less than £60,000 in a bid to find a way to overcome the effects of skill shortages and rising building costs. Having entered the competition with two consortia neither of bptw's submissions were eventually chosen but both were highly commended for the way in which their entries proved that the challenge was achievable through the implementation of design innovation, partnering and construction efficiency; all intrinsic principles of the best practice outlined by John Egan almost a decade earlier.

Perceived as a valuable experience that influenced thinking on the bidding teams future work, it was however inevitable that the unrealistic market demands of the competition would be hard pressed to apply to daily practice. For bptw, the Design to Manufacture commendation would be fast usurped by several award-winning bptw partnership schemes that alternately embodied the increasingly diverse mix of housing needs, the complexity of tenure and design that challenged the cost benefits and efficiency of the modern construction system, and conversely, bptw's efforts to maximise the full potential of the MMC systems where most appropriate.

Continuing to apply itself to the type of regeneration projects that had helped establish its reputation as an integrity-led community-focussed practice, bptw was appointed to deliver the regeneration of the Sundermead Estate, later known as River Mill Park, adjoining Lewisham town centre and railway station in South London.

River Mill Park with the naturalised River Ravensbourne in front.

Particularly benefiting from the location of an adjoining redundant council depot, the project was undertaken as a phased redevelopment programme, the former depot site developed as the first phase enabling residents to move from existing to new homes in a single transfer. The second phase subsequently developed when existing homes had been vacated and demolished.

Community consultation remained central to the project, and through close working with the residents of the estate, the project proved opportune for the introduction of the home-zone concept; incorporating pedestrian-friendly street principles, and successfully demonstrating how sometimes arbitrary planning standards, such as back-to-back distances could be adapted to enable wider frontage homes to be provided and a more satisfactory outcome for the community.

Residents were also consulted regarding the height of the development and despite their initial pre-conceptions, based on judgement of the former four storey maisonettes of the Sundermead Estate, they tested and eventually endorsed 'flatted' accommodation, of between six and eight storeys, that they perceived would exploit River Mill Park's unique location overlooking surrounding green space.

At the same time, and following on from the Peckham Partnership project, bptw in conjunction with PTEa were appointed by the London Borough of Southwark to deliver the regeneration of the Elmington Estate in Camberwell, South London. Involving a multi-phased redevelopment that will eventually provide around 300 homes the transformation of a largely dysfunctional estate, the first phase of the development was to demonstrate the practice's maturity in its approach to urban planning and to become bptw's first exemplar scheme to achieve the Commission for Architecture and the Built Environment (CABE) Silver Standard award in 2005. Having met the award criteria on the grounds of aesthetics, accessibility, safety and inclusiveness, in addition to the design of the external and internal space, it was a welcome testimony to the success of bptw's holistic approach to urban development, and their commitment to the wider issues of community design.

Remaining one of bptw's most defining projects to date, the redevelopment of the Pepys Estate in Deptford, South London gained the same CABE Silver Standard the year following Elmington, having in the meantime already achieved Housing Design Award's Exhibition of Excellence commendation and Brick Awards recognition as Best Public Housing Development, both received in the same year.

Appointed as lead designer on the project after winning a publicly judged masterplanning competition for the proposed development of the Pepys Estate, bptw worked in close collaboration with Hyde Housing Association to deliver the eventual provision of over 280 new mixed-tenure affordable homes across the four phases of the estate. A site of vast contradiction, Pepys not only incorporated widespread pockets of social and economic deprivation, with the anti-social characteristics and criminal activity typically associated with failing 1960s designed urban estates, but also a unique position adjacent to the River Thames, considerable areas of surrounding green space and the incorporation of a number of Grade II listed former Admiralty office buildings. Sustainability therefore became of chief importance over the regeneration of the estate.

Returning to bptw's extensive research and development into the potential for modern methods of construction to work effectively in affordable housing schemes, the practice, in close conjunction

Opposite: Phase one of the completed Pepys Estate which was designed to reflect the characteristics of the Grade II listed former Admiralty office buildings incorporated into the overall redevelopment.

with Rydon Construction, worked to deliver a timber frame solution that would prove energy and time-efficient whilst not compromising the overall design of the scheme. Eventually engaging specialist suppliers, the timber frame solution was used on the first and third phases of the development; implemented, in the latter instance, for a seven-storey apartment; a decision that pushed the capacity of the technology to almost unprecedented levels.

Thereby drawing the first five years of the new millennium to a close, the two projects came to consolidate bptw's vision to implement cost effective, meaningful and exemplary design, while also marking the practice's successful transition to the role of lead masterplanner and designer of large scale affordable housing schemes. Notably however, neither Pepys, nor Elmington were driven by iconic agendas, but by the surrounding context of local buildings and their individual neighbourhood communities. Both award-winning projects in their own right, the success of the two schemes were also undoubtedly major contributors to bptw's own 'Architectural Practice' accolade of the same year. They were similarly testament to the practice's ability to enable the provision of high quality social housing that, even on a limited budget, was to the quality of best practice in any sector, irrespective of the method of construction.

Elmington

While adjunct to the Peckham Partnership project and funded through the extension of the same Single Regeneration Budget initiative from the London Borough of Southwark, the £8.8 million masterplaning and multi-phased redevelopment of the Elmington Estate in Camberwell, South London, was a particularly distinctive scheme in its own right; an exemplar of bptw's maturity in their approach to urban planning and the practice's first project to achieve the Commission for Architecture and the Built Environment (CABE) Silver Standard award in 2005.

Already joint masterplanners and designers for the consortia selected to develop the five Peckham estates, bptw partnership and Pollard Thomas Edwards architects were appointed in 1999 by the London Borough of Southwark to produce a masterplan for the redevelopment of Elmington and were subsequently appointed by the contractors, Countryside Properties. Their scheme achieved planning approval in May of the following year and construction of the new development was already underway in January 2002.

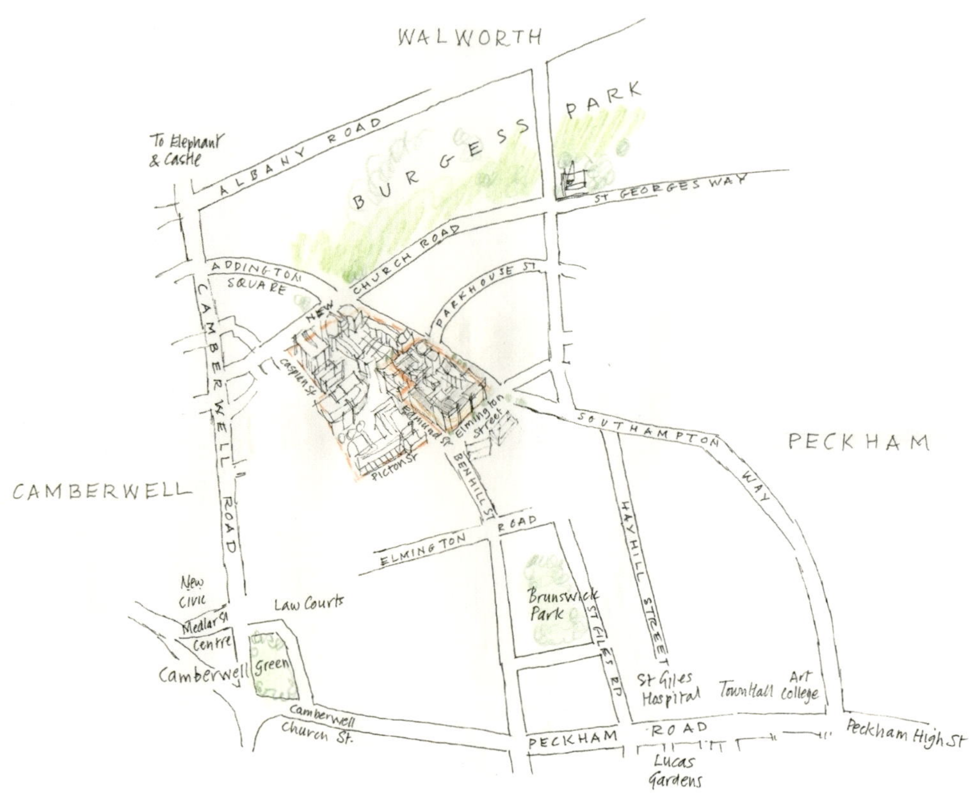

Aiming to transform the Camberwell neighbourhood, contemporaneously identified as the fifth most deprived ward in the country with serious safety concerns into a community with new opportunities and a heightened sense of security and civic pride, the two practices collaborated to provide almost 300 new homes on the former site of the Elmington Estate which comprised, four high-rise 'slab' blocks with inherent structural weaknesses and medium-rise maisonette blocks that were initially developed in the 1960s.

Subsequently, proposing the demolition and replacement of the former estate with a mix of medium-rise apartment buildings and terrace houses, including one and two bedroom flats, and two, three, four and five bedroom houses, the urban regeneration plan for Elmington was developed with the aim of reinstating a traditional Victorian street pattern, providing safer

Opposite top: Elmington Estate, Camberwell
Opposite bottom: View of the typical street level bicycle and refuse storage space provided for each house.
Above: Early proposals for the redevelopment, focussing on the design of the street frontage and main pedestrian thoroughfare.

pedestrian route and increased access to outdoor areas in the effort to remedy the largely dysfunctional public realm, the prevalent criminality, poor access and socio-economic decline. The new homes addressed a range of affordable housing needs for families, couples and those with varying degree of mobility and while most were retained for rent by Southwark Borough Council, a small proportion were released for private sale, reinforcing in the process the quality and future commercial potential of the regeneration project.

Developed in two phases, with incremental stages built into the programme to avoid moving residents twice, for instance, phase one provided approximately 100 new homes that were built in advance of the demolition and slotted into spaces between the old blocks while phase two saw the completion of the network of streets with private gardens in the interior of the blocks, the entirety of the Elmington redevelopment was significantly led by extensive consultation with the local residents.

Involving meetings held after working hours and on weekends, frequent mail-shots and local progress updates in addition to post-occupancy evaluations, the consultation process also involved each of the households of the former neighbourhood being given the option of moving to the new council homes being redeveloped on the Elmington Estate or other properties elsewhere in the borough. Prioritising those who wished to stay on the estate, future residents of the new build homes were able to play an active role in the design of their homes, for example, through the selection of additional features such as water butts that they wished to be incorporated into their properties. Built to Lifetime Homes Standards, it was also significant that the homes being built as part of the Elmington project generally provided larger kitchens and bathrooms than the old flats, and gave many residents their own garden for the first time.

Reinforcing this new sense of pride in the 'newness' of the redevelopment, the overall regeneration plan sought to re-establish a new feeling of pride in the community and a connected network of residential homes that would relate to their surrounding streetscape and through greater interaction with the street frontage, provide safe pedestrian routes and heightened passive security, supported throughout by the application of Secured by Design principles. Thereby, both the masterplan and first phase of the development responded to the surrounding Victorian style of housing and street patterns with the chief aim of integrating the residential neighbourhood into the community and removing the social stigma of a monolithic and alienated estate.

Influenced by traditional residential neighbourhoods where terrace form houses would be punctuated by higher rise residences or buildings such as shops or pubs accommodating amenities for common interaction and public uses; the layout of the new Elmington development, and the design of stronger, more defined street corners particularly, mirrored this in the effort to design-in an increased level of physical and social resident contact, a firmer sense of architectural identity, and to provide people with a revitalised sense of belonging and community. Reinforcing this, the corner apartment buildings also act as gateways to key pedestrian thoroughfares and shared public spaces while thresholds to all of the houses are level with the street and feature front and rear gardens of varying size, each providing space for bicycle and refuse storage. All apartments have private balconies.

Above: Illustrating the use of the corner building as a pedestrian gateway, reinforced by the parallel curve of the brick landscaping feature.
Opposite top: Sensitive planting and additional landscape features particularly add to the sense of a high quality public realm.
Opposite bottom left: Site plan showing final layout of the completed site.
Opposite bottom right: Elevation of a three storey block.

Left: Streets reflect the development's Victorian design influences with conventional layout patterns arranged along long sweeping curves with defined corners and decorative brickwork features.
Opposite left: Ensuring maximised security, car parking bays are located directly outside communal entrances and overlooked by residential properties to ensure passive surveillance.
Opposite right: Rear view of the houses showing private access.

Heightening the sense of a neighbourhood identity, each of the residential blocks have the same architectural style and use the same range of materials throughout the two phases. Throughout the scheme, the recurring use of the mono-pitched roof adds a greater sense of scale to routes through the estate, particularly befitting the cul-de-sacs, short streets and shared pedestrian and vehicular surfaces that feature throughout the new development; prioritising the pedestrian via careful layout design and a range of inherent traffic control measures. Simultaneously, recognising the high importance residents place on being able to overlook their cars, parking space has been allocated in designated parking courts and in open, landscaped areas that are well lit and overlooked by residential properties to ensure passive surveillance.

Responding to the need of robust and thermally efficient properties, reducing maintenance and management issues and providing a long-term housing solution, brick and concrete construction constitutes the core of the scheme. Combining matching red and yellow bricks with grey roofs and metalwork for balconies, feature elements are highlighted in green glazed bricks and cream coloured render, while stack bonding and decorative formations provide additional articulation to the brickwork. The scheme also features steel balconies, render and timber panelling and in accordance with its design influences, contains details typical in decorative features of Victorian homes including the use of parapets, curved walls and railings.

These details, combined with high quality landscape materials and additional features that enhance the public realm, such as the provision of strategically placed outdoor seating and attractive and inviting communal entrances, collectively add to the Elmington's capacity to function as a well designed, carefully maintained and community-focused urban neighbourhood.

Five Steps Nursery

Delivered through the wider Single Regeneration Budget funded redevelopment of the Silwood Estate situated on the joint border between the London Boroughs of Lewisham and Southwark, South London; Five Steps Nursery was completed and officially opened to the public in 2006. Responding to the consultation feedback outlining the specific needs of the local community, the childcare and education centre provides vital support for parents on the Silwood Estate and eight of the 32 spaces available at the nursery are prioritised for children with particular needs such as disabilities, learning difficulties, or for those with an isolated or asylum seeker family background.

An integral part of the masterplan produced by bptw partnership for the wider redevelopment of the estate, which following an extensive consultation process, includes the provision of new-build housing and community amenity facilities, bptw were appointed to provide the pre-planning services by the London Borough of Lewisham and post-contract design for the Nursery by Higgins Construction in 2003.

An L-shaped building, situated on a street corner adjacent to Silwood Pocket Park and within the context of a large scale, new-build residential community of 600 homes, primarily comprising of low-rise houses and medium-rise apartment blocks, the design for Five Steps Nursery inevitably focussed on prioritising the safety and privacy of the children's outdoor play space, while allowing the nursery to establish a presence within the local community.

Opposite: Site plan showing ground floor layout and external landscape plans.
Above: The exterior of the nursery showing the main entrance.

Above: Original sketch elevations showing the scheme from each aspect.
Opposite: Interior classroom view highlighting the focus on natural light and stimulating coloured walls.

In response to the needs of the teachers, information and service providers in addition to the requirements for external and internal play areas, the design for the Nursery also incorporated internal space for teaching, care, offices and a reception for the centre. Utilising the potential of the building's position, this space was designed into the external corner blocks, forming a natural barrier between the street and the concealed play area and garden inside.

Simultaneously ensuring a degree of interaction between the nursery and the streetscape, a prominent circular drum designed to mark the corner of the block helped the centre to become a distinct part of the community's architectural landscape. Warm, pale coloured render and timber panelling feature at the secure entrance of the building, as well as on the drum, while alternating stripes of brick have been used along the teaching and office wings.

Internally, the teaching spaces and offices benefit from natural light with windows overlooking the street. Exposed timber beams accentuate the sloping roof, and rooms have been designed to allow for flexible adaptation in size and space to accommodate the children's varying needs. Allowing a strong sense of interactivity between the teaching and play areas, corridors lead directly between the internal rooms and external landscaping and the soft play area is immediately beside sheltered

supervision space for the protection and comfort of both teachers and children. Externally decorated with vibrantly coloured shaped design, the cushioned rubber flooring was specified to accommodate a range of play equipment and naturally merges with wider landscaped garden space marking the perimeter of the Nursery.

Testament to the success of Five Steps Nursery and the quality of its functionality and aesthetic appeal as perceived by local residents and end users within the community, bptw were later appointed by London & Quadrant to design the mixed-use Silwood Community Centre, which included 33 homes, office space, IT suites, landscaped space and a community play area. Mirroring the strength of the Nursery's design, the Community Centre's main building would similarly provide a strong street frontage for the wider community, including a vibrant entrance articulated with coloured glazing and render and a dynamic roof structure to assimilate the development with the new-build architecture of bptw's original masterplan for the Silwood area.

Top: Strips of alternating coloured brick have been used to indicate the different internal uses of the building.
Bottom: The distinctive circular cream drum of the Nursery provides internal office space for the Nursery's administrative offices.
Opposite: View of the enclosed outdoor play area in use.

Northumberland Park Neighbourhood Resource Centre

Funded through the JUNP (Joining up Northumberland Park) SRB programme, the £1.6 million Northumberland Park Neighbourhood Resource Centre, opened in 2004 by Lord Rooker, former Minister for Regeneration, was a core focal point of the wider regeneration of the Northumberland Park and White Hart Lane neighbourhood in Tottenham, North London.

Situated in the Heart of Park Lane, yards from Tottenham Hotspur football ground, the Resource Centre's local ward was classified among the 5 per cent most deprived wards in England in the government's 2000 Indices of Deprivation, scoring particularly poorly in terms of educational achievement and child poverty. The design brief for the project subsequently focussed on addressing these specific issues; requiring a functional, purpose-built development that would serve as a lasting professional resource while maintaining an imaginative aesthetic appeal that would attract the use of the local community. Testifying to the ultimate fulfilment of this brief, the completed scheme became part of the Open House London programme in 2005, pinpointed as an exemplar of welcoming and stimulating design for learning and community development.

Appointed as architects and employers agent for the project in 2001, bptw worked in close consultation with local residents and clients, London Borough of Haringey and Newlon Housing Trust, to develop the community resource facility on the site of a derelict shopping precinct, podium and a number of disused and dangerous underground garages which had become a local epicentre of anti-social behaviour and criminal activity. Notably, the innovative reuse of existing materials from the former garage buildings would later provide an energy efficient solution throughout the construction and use of the Resource Centre, while helping minimise disruption to the surrounding residential community.

Focussing on designing-out the opportunities for criminal behaviour, while creating an inspirational and active streetscape that would encourage community interaction and the passive surveillance of those using the Centre, bptw, working with contractors, Diamond Build, prioritised the demolition of the podium, creating in its place landscaped external areas and allowing the introduction of natural light and ventilation to the lower level of the Resource Centre. Maximising the effectiveness of this, a lightwell atrium and sunpipe, enhanced with brightly coloured finishes and reflective surfaces, have been used to channel further natural light into areas concealed from natural solar gain. Contemporary finishes and full-height glazing at the front entrance similarly help meet the aspiration for transparency and openness while creating a strong street frontage for the building.

Befitting the internal use of the building, the design naturally supported the provision of recreational, reception and meeting space on the lower floor with office space on the higher levels used to provide essential community services from agencies including Sure Start, Neighbourhood Wardens, Learn Direct, Kinesis and a number of Primary Care Trust plus services, all of which directly targeted the local community's most prevalent social problems. The Centre has proved a popular and well-used resource since its opening and achieved the title of 'Best Community Building' at the Haringey Design Awards in 2006.

Opposite top: Side elevation showing view of the Centre from Rothbury Walk. *Opposite bottom*: The Resource Centre in the early stages of construction.

neighbourhood centre

THAMES BOOKMAKERS
THAMES
BOOKMAKERS

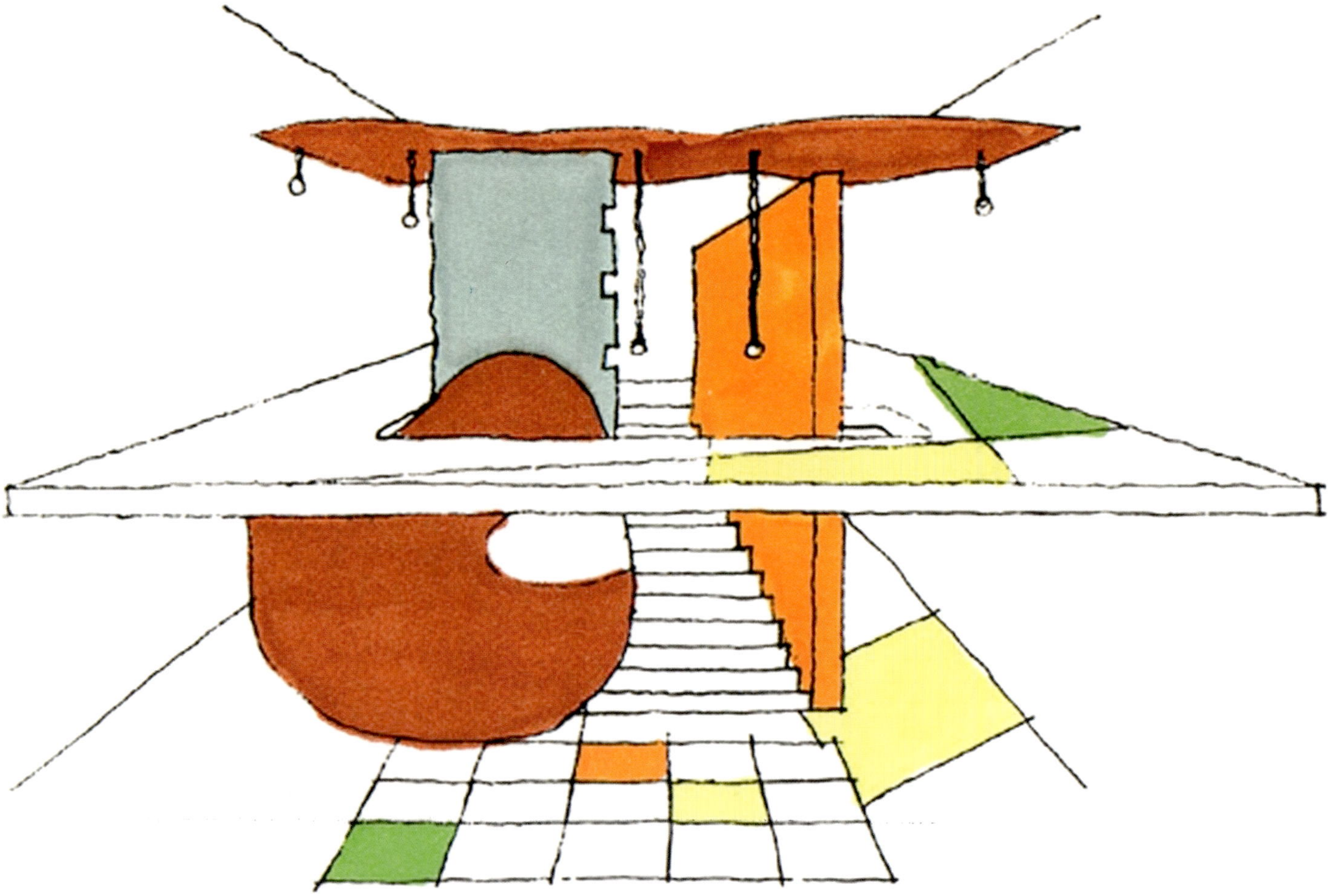

Above: Early concept sketch providing a cross section of the Centre's reception area and second floor.
Bottom: Northumberland Park Neighbourhood Resource Centre, post-completion.
Opposite: View of the atrium and the use of colour and reflective surface material to create a bright, vibrant and welcoming internal environment.

Pepys

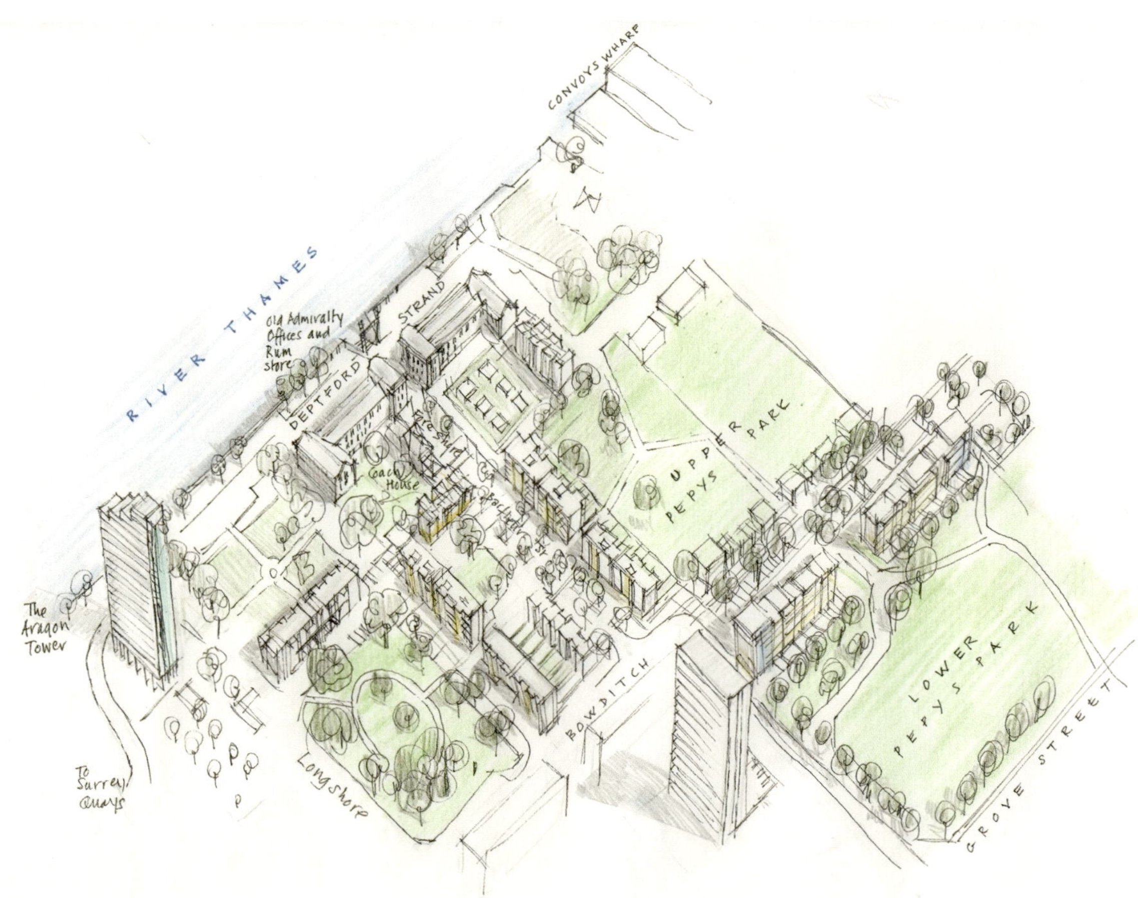

Alongside Evelyn and Milton Court, the Pepys Estate in Deptford, South London became the third significant regeneration scheme in the London Borough of Lewisham to simultaneously follow on from Estate Action funded improvements in the late 1990s. However, unprecedented in scale and topographical variation, the redevelopment of the former problem estate into a Building for Life Silver award winning environment became one of bptw's most defining projects to date. Completed in 2007, the regeneration scheme also achieved Brick Awards title of *Best Public Housing Development* and the Housing Design Award's *Exhibition of Excellence* commendation in 2005.

Having already benefited from earlier refurbishment work including the full refurbishment of 8 identical blocks of maisonette flats prior to 2002, further work across the remainder of the Pepys Estate was due to be undertaken before the London Borough of Lewisham made the decision to carry out the complete demolition and redevelopment of five previously unimproved blocks on the estate, transferring the management of the housing stock to Hyde Housing Association. Notably, the 26 storey Aragon Tower Block was concurrently sold to Berkeley Homes and later redeveloped for private sale.

The ensuing design competition and public exhibition for the masterplan of the proposed redevelopment of the Pepys Estate, run by Hyde and judged by residents of the estate and representatives from the local authority, saw the selection of bptw's submission over

Left: Pepys Estate, Deptford.
Right and opposite top: Photographs of Pepys prior to the estate's regeneration, focussing on the concrete-surfaced podium and undercroft areas and derelict car parking provision.
Opposite middle: Polystyrene model used to demonstrate the proposed layout of the scheme throughout the design process
Opposite bottom: Sketch of the winning masterplan outlining the original plans for the overall redevelopment of the Pepys Estate.

two alternative proposals and, procured through a PPC 2000 project partnering contract, the practice's subsequent appointment as lead designer and masterplanner for the project.

Working in close collaboration with Hyde Housing Association and subsequently the selected contractor, Rydon Construction, the masterplan for the redevelopment of the Pepys Estate would eventually deliver 285 new mixed-tenure affordable homes comprising a range of flats and family houses across four phases of the Estate. At the forefront of the regeneration process from its inception, the local community played a significant role in influencing fundamental decisions over the design of the site and the long term management of the Estate's assets, including the incorporation of a number of Grade II listed former Admiralty office buildings which comprised an integral part of the Estate's legacy as a Royal Dockyards site. Adding to the inherent contradiction within the neighbourhood, in contrast to Pepys' uniquely historic position adjacent to the River Thames the Estate also incorporated the anti-social characteristics and latent criminal activity typically associated with the failure of socially and economically deprived failing 1960s-designed urban estates.

Subsequently, while the initial design stages required close liaison with English Heritage to develop solutions sensitive to the Grade II listed dockyard buildings, extensive community consultation was simultaneously carried out, even prior to bptw's selection as lead designer, to identify the main areas of resident concern over the Estate's physical environment. Emerging from the results of the Estate-wide survey, chief problems included the poor quality and confusing pedestrian routes through the Estate, the lack of ground level accommodation and private gardens and concurrently, the poor accessibility overall with steps and ramps to raised public areas. The bleak, extensively concrete-surfaced podium and undercroft areas were similarly

perceived as features particularly susceptible to the encouragement of crime and anti-social behaviour, as were the derelict underground car parking areas, problematic entrance halls and extensive horizontal walkways between individual apartments.

Focussing on designing-out these features and creating newly accessible, inter-connected public spaces, capitalising on the Estate's relation to the River Thames and the surrounding green space; further to their appointment as masterplanners for the project, bptw worked in close collaboration with the resident-led Steering Committee for Pepys Estate Action which was formed in January 2000. Over the course of the following 12 months 22 joint meetings were held, bringing to the fore a number of challenges including issues of poor housing management and fundamentally, the community's reluctance to accept bptw's initial proposals for the reconfiguration of the residential blocks and existing green space on the estate. Taking this into account, the practice adapted their proposals to work from the footprint of the original buildings.

Comprised of three larger phases, providing a mix of larger family homes and one, two, and three bedroom flats and a fourth phase, consisting of eight four and five bedroom houses for shared ownership and affordable rent, each part of the site has a distinct

Above: Entrance to the main stair core (phase one). Featuring a mix of stock brick, timber panelling and striking glazing, the communal entryways contribute to the building's visual appeal, while allowing for heightened community interaction.
Opposite top right: Elevations for phase one, block E family houses. Front elevation, top, with rear view below.
Opposite bottom: View of phase one family houses (featuring stock brick and pale render) with the Grade II listed former Admiralty offices behind.

Opposite top: Side view of Pepys phase three, punctuated by clear canopies and the use of galvanised steel.
Opposite bottom: Phase one; Granite-effect paving complements the original cobblestones surrounding the historic buildings, while overlooked pathways provide safe and level thoroughfares to connected open spaces.
Left and top right: Interior views from phases one and three. Interior size specifications exceed minimum Lifetime Home Standards and principal living areas are largely south-facing, maximising their passive solar orientation.
Bottom right: Rear of phase two, facing Admiralty Square where newly planted London Plane Trees enhance the existing landscape and the views to the river through the lower level of the building.

theme and care was taken to ensure the connection between the residential neighbourhood, the surrounding community and the planned future development at Convoy's Wharf. The development of phase two, for instance, required particular consultation with English Heritage and its warehouse-influenced design serves to link the new residential apartments with the remaining Grade II listed buildings that remain from the Admiralty offices. Paved pathways link with the cobbled streets surrounding the listed buildings and continue through to the open public space within the Pepys Estate while allowing for open views through the centre of the apartment buildings to the river.

Across the remaining phases of the scheme, selected building materials predominantly included the use of London stock brick and textured timber panelling on the elevations of the apartment blocks and houses. In common with the approach taken at the contemporaneously designed mixed-tenure Joseph Tritton scheme in Battersea, the entrances are marked by strong timber and glazing elements with clear elegant canopies and the materials on the main elevations are punctuated by galvanised steel and timber balconies, softened by pale rendering.

Phase one, comprising of seven family houses and 120 flats, is particularly significant for the way in

which its design emphasises the creation of a vertical access solution as opposed to the long, anonymous horizontal walkways and faceless central entrances prevalent on the former Estate. With the new facade established through the division of the apartment blocks into small groups of flats, arranged around stair cores served by individual entrances and accessed at each level of the building, the rearrangement of the buildings significantly allowed for increased interaction between neighbours, a more communal street frontage. Further to specific resident requests, the interior design and layout of the buildings were developed to meet the same generous size specifications of the original flats which considerably exceeded minimum Lifetime Home Standards. A key feature of the existing flats, highlighted in the consultation process, the new apartments were designed to provide dual aspect orientation and all principal living areas were designed to maximise their passive solar orientation, avoiding a north-facing aspect wherever possible.

Similarly contributing to the project's Eco-Homes 'very good' rating, Pepys was constructed using modern methods of construction, and timber frame technology specifically, on the first and third phases of the development. Implemented for a seven storey apartment as part of phase three, this pushed the capacity of the technology to almost unprecedented levels, reflecting the

innovation with which the whole project was executed. Further heightening the cost and environmental-effectiveness of the redevelopment, the scheme also used the crushed concrete from the demolition of the raised walkways, undercroft areas and run-down garages for the extensive re-levelling of the site overall.

Thereby helping to consolidate bptw's vision for the Estate as an exemplar of cost-effective, meaningful and responsible design, the completion of the Pepys redevelopment and its widely recognised success was testament to bptw's capacity to produce award-winning architecture for the social housing sector that, irrespective of budget constraints and without being driven by any iconic agenda, was to the quality of best practice in any sector.

Opposite: Phase one of the completed Pepys Estate which was designed to reflect the characteristics of the Grade II listed former Admiralty office buildings incorporated into the overall redevelopment.
Left: Preliminary visualisation of Pepys phase two, view from river, northeast of the building.
Right: Designed to home-zone principles, the newly levelled public areas promote pedestrian, disabled and pushchair access, prioritising the needs of people over cars.

The Laurels Healthy Living Centre & Turners Court

Completed in 2004, The Laurels Healthy Living Centre was a landmark project for both the local community and bptw, serving as the first major mixed-use scheme to be undertaken by the practice.

Required to provide an innovative and holistic approach to community development, bptw were appointed in 2001 as architects for the £8 million project, which would eventually comprise of a new local resource building combining 71 shared ownership and affordable rented homes with a 1,500 square metre facility accommodating health resources for the local community.

Situated within a New Deal for Communities (NDC) area, on a prominent corner block in Tottenham, North London, the scheme was originally targeted as a major community regeneration project and was developed by the local NDC, the London Borough of Haringey and Circle 33 Housing Trust, in close conjunction with the local Primary Care Trust.

Incorporating the mixed affordable rent and privately owned homes in four and five storey buildings arranged on the levels above the ground floor Healthy Living Centre and in a separate building accessed from the street frontage, The Laurels also accommodates several General Practitioner surgeries which are fully compliant for disabled access, in addition to a range of community health projects funded by The Bridge NDC including health advocacy, counselling, complementary therapies, a Citizens Advice Bureau and a community cafe, designed to provide training and employment opportunities as well as servicing the staff and the local community. A significant indicator of the future drawing towards mixed-use developments and their success in fulfilling the requirements of the urban community, the initiative was quickly noted for the way it revitalised the adjacent Chestnuts Park neighbourhood and became a starting point for nearby high quality redevelopment of the local hospital site and industrial area.

Opposite left: The Laurels Healthy Living Centre & Turners Court, Tottenham. Opposite right: View of the rear of the Health Centre, showing the landscaped courtyard and panelled glazing. *Above*: Illustrating the prominence of the building's size and shape against the primarily low-rise streetscape of St Ann's Road.

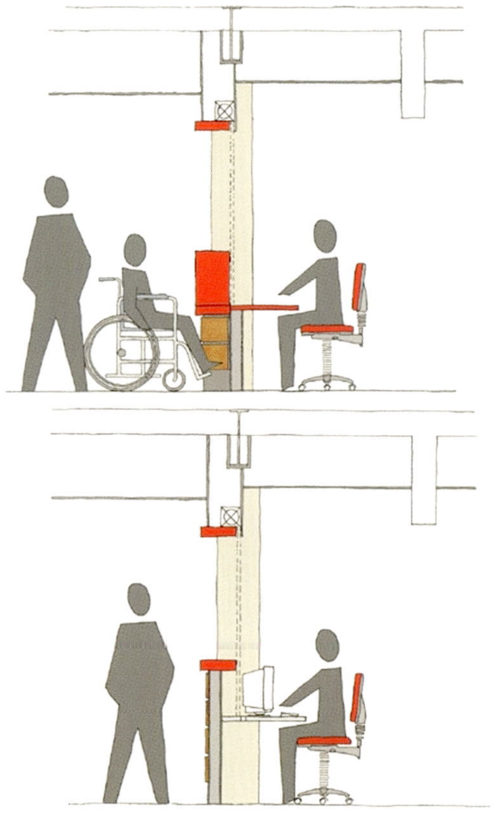

Opposite left: External fins marking the stairway entrance to the residential units.
Opposite top right: Preliminary visualisation of the surgeries internal layout.
Opposite bottom right: Simple cross section of the Heath Centre, which is fully compliant for disabled access.
Right: View showing higher residential storeys over the ground floor community facilities.

Highlighting bptw's capacity to adapt their conventional consultative procedures to new-build and commercial-use developments, while retaining their focus on the needs of the end user and the local community, the success of the Laurels Healthy Living Centre & Turners Courts was in no small part attributable to the major consultation process undertaken with the local health care provider, Circle 33 Housing Trust, and the London Borough of Haringey. Building on the practice's earlier experience of community regeneration despite being unable to directly engage with the eventual tenants of the new-build homes, bptw also placed a significant investment in the views of the residents who would ultimately neighbour the proposed development. Local people were therefore engaged with throughout the design and construction process, and in addition to local exhibitions, bptw also arranged drop-in sessions to discuss the proposals and leafleted almost 500 local homes prior to planning approval being granted in March 2002.

The outcome of such extensive consultation would also influence the final design of the scheme, contributing to both the preferred layout of the development in addition to its aesthetic impact on the local area; both elements that had been largely determined through bptw's interior and exterior photorealistic visualisations which were used to communicate the proposed designs.

The new building was ultimately designed with distinctive and boldly coloured vertical fins fronting onto the street, adding a new vibrancy to the streetscape of St Anne's Road, while the rear of the building is defined by panelled glazing overlooking a landscaped courtyard. A pale London stock brick has been used throughout the scheme, contrasting with the orange fins which define stairway entrances and are straddled by white render boxed balconies throughout the residential section. Blue render feature walls were meanwhile used to signify the healthcare use in other sections of the project.

Testifying to the overall success of the scheme, the development won the 'Best Partnership and Contribution to Regeneration' category of the 2004 Affordable Home Ownership Awards run by the National Housing Federation and gained considerable social and political acclaim as a national example of best practice.

Above: Visualisation of the early external designs for the Healthy Living Centre.
Opposite: Internal view of the health care reception area.

Main
Reception
Reception-Information

Ordsall Estate

With the objective of bringing the Ordsall Estate in line with the extensive development contemporaneously taking place in the area, encouraging growth in terms of the community's living and communal facilities and its integration with other parts of the city, bptw were appointed by Salford City Council and Legendary Property Company (LPC) to deliver the masterplan and framework for development for the Salford Estate in 2004.

The product of an opportune phone call, provoked by hearsay of LPC's search for a practice willing to meet their ambitious criteria for tower block refurbishment, and a resultant meeting between bptw and the local authority establishing their mutual commitment to the fundamental improvement of the public realm in the context of extensive consultation with residents and key stakeholders; bptw's appointment on the Ordsall scheme afforded the practice the opportunity to have a formative impact on an area with considerable development potential.

Situated between two areas of relative wealth; the extensively revitalised commercial area of Manchester City centre and the newly regenerated Salford Quays; and effectively separated from them through the bindings of three major roads and the Manchester Ship Canal, the decline of local industry and the poorly connected routes through the estate to surrounding parks, transport hubs and high quality public amenities, had seen the increasing isolation of the Ordsall Estate and its subsequent decline in terms of deprivation and the social, economic and environmental issues faced by the local community.

Left: Site plan highlighting Ordsall Estate and its geographical relation to Manchester City Centre and Salford Quays.
Opposite: The Ordsall masterplan, outlining proposals for the new buildings, amenity areas and existing landmarks.

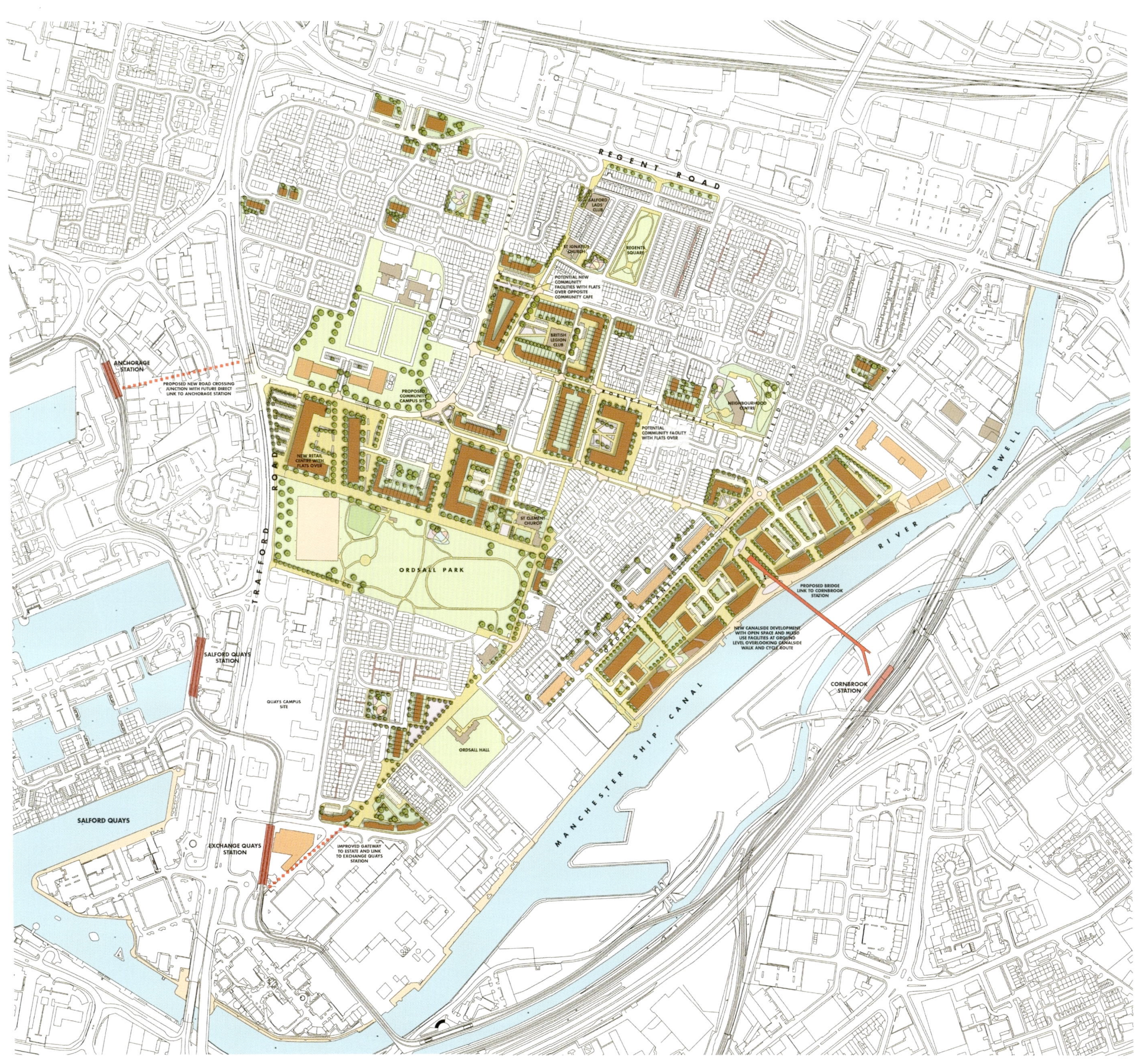
REGENT ROAD
SALFORD LADS CLUB
ST IGNATIUS CHURCH
REGENTS SQUARE
POTENTIAL NEW COMMUNITY FACILITIES WITH FLATS OVER OPPOSITE COMMUNITY CAFE
BRITISH LEGION CLUB
ANCHORAGE STATION
PROPOSED NEW ROAD CROSSING JUNCTION WITH FUTURE DIRECT LINK TO ANCHORAGE STATION
PROPOSED COMMUNITY CAMPUS SITE
NEIGHBOURHOOD CENTRE
POTENTIAL COMMUNITY FACILITY WITH FLATS OVER
NEW RETAIL CENTRE WITH FLATS OVER
TRAFFORD ROAD
ST CLEMENT CHURCH
ORDSALL PARK
RIVER IRWELL
PROPOSED BRIDGE LINK TO CORNBROOK STATION
NEW CANALSIDE DEVELOPMENT WITH OPEN SPACE AND MIXED USE FACILITIES AT GROUND LEVEL OVERLOOKING CANALSIDE WALK AND CYCLE ROUTE
SALFORD QUAYS STATION
CORNBROOK STATION
QUAYS CAMPUS SITE
ORDSALL HALL
MANCHESTER SHIP CANAL
SALFORD QUAYS
EXCHANGE QUAYS STATION
IMPROVED GATEWAY TO ESTATE AND LINK TO EXCHANGE QUAYS STATION

In addition to wider analysis of the area, bptw's masterplan was significantly informed by an extensive consultation process involving public exhibitions, written questionnaires and surveys and walking audits of the estate with Ordsall residents, key stakeholders, developers and local councillors. While invaluable in terms of the general insight it provided into local perception and key access needs, the audits were particularly useful for their role in separating well-used routes from alleyways which would ideally be gated, and pleasant open spaces from areas where anti-social behaviour was fostered.

Appositely, the consultation process identified several features that were a source of considerable community pride. Including Ordsall Hall, an Elizabethan Manor set within its own grounds and Monmouth Park, an area of open green space at the gateway of the Estate, both features were duly incorporated as integral parts of the final masterplan.

Conversely, main roads flanked by the backs of houses which prevented any natural surveillance were noted as being of particular concern, as was the demise of the district centre, the former economic hub of the Estate; the canal and the disused and derelict warehouses along its bank, which had become one of the most significant problem areas, proving both structurally unsafe and a vulnerable base for criminal misuse and anti-social behaviour. Dealing with these concerns, the masterplan proposed that safety issues were addressed with improved lighting, a designed-in active street frontage with natural surveillance from overlooking properties and the identification of key pedestrian and traffic routes through the Estate, connecting the residential community with public squares, avenues running parallel to parks and easily accessible transport links. Maximising the commercial appeal of waterside properties, the masterplan also outlined the development of homes overlooking the River Irwell which would become a significant focus area for the regeneration of the Estate.

Providing options appraisal and feasibility studies for the Ordsall Estate masterplan, bptw proposed the development of 1,000 new dwellings for the Estate and its surrounding area, along with a new health centre and community facilities, significant landscape improvements to the existing parks and additional play areas throughout the estate.

The connection between the Ordsall Estate community and the wider economic and civic hub, including Manchester City Centre, Salford Quays and Castlefield will also be achieved through the introduction of new pedestrian and cycle routes in addition to improved accessibility to local Metrolink stations.

Top and middle: Images of the Ordsall Estate, before regeneration.
Bottom: Consultation design boards for the proposed Ordsall scheme.
Opposite: Resident consultation boards showing design plans for the Ordsall Estate.

Joseph Tritton

Located on the site of the former Joseph Tritton School in Battersea, the £9 million new-build residential development, completed in 2005, was designed to respond to the changing demographic of the London Borough of Wandsworth; specifically, to the mixed-tenure housing needs created by the rising numbers of aspiring new home owners moving into the increasingly popular South London residential area.

With an objective to optimise the use of the former school quad, positioning each of the buildings around a green landscaped space while maintaining a strong street frontage that reflected the scale of the surrounding area, bptw were appointed by Threshold Housing to provide 131 affordable new homes, including flats and maisonettes, available for rent, supported housing and shared ownership.

Working closely with the housing association, Local Authority and the Battersea community, bptw carried out an extensive consultation process, including participation in a series of evening events that were held to gain feedback from residents and local stakeholders on needs within the development and on the proposals overall. Supported by the contractor, Higgins, bptw subsequently designed a housing scheme that worked harmoniously with the surrounding buildings and the historical context of the area, while providing a robust, energy efficient and high quality housing solution that belies the commonly held visual perception of social housing.

Taking advantage of the scale of the Joseph Tritton quad, the seven new blocks of the development surrounds two large landscaped courtyards. Arranged in three wings that meet at a corner axis punctuated by stair cores, the three to five storey apartment blocks have a strong brick street frontage punctuated by sleek, galvanised steel and glass balconies. In addition to accentuating the exterior of the housing scheme, the balconies also add a sense of spaciousness to the upper floor flats and, highlighted by

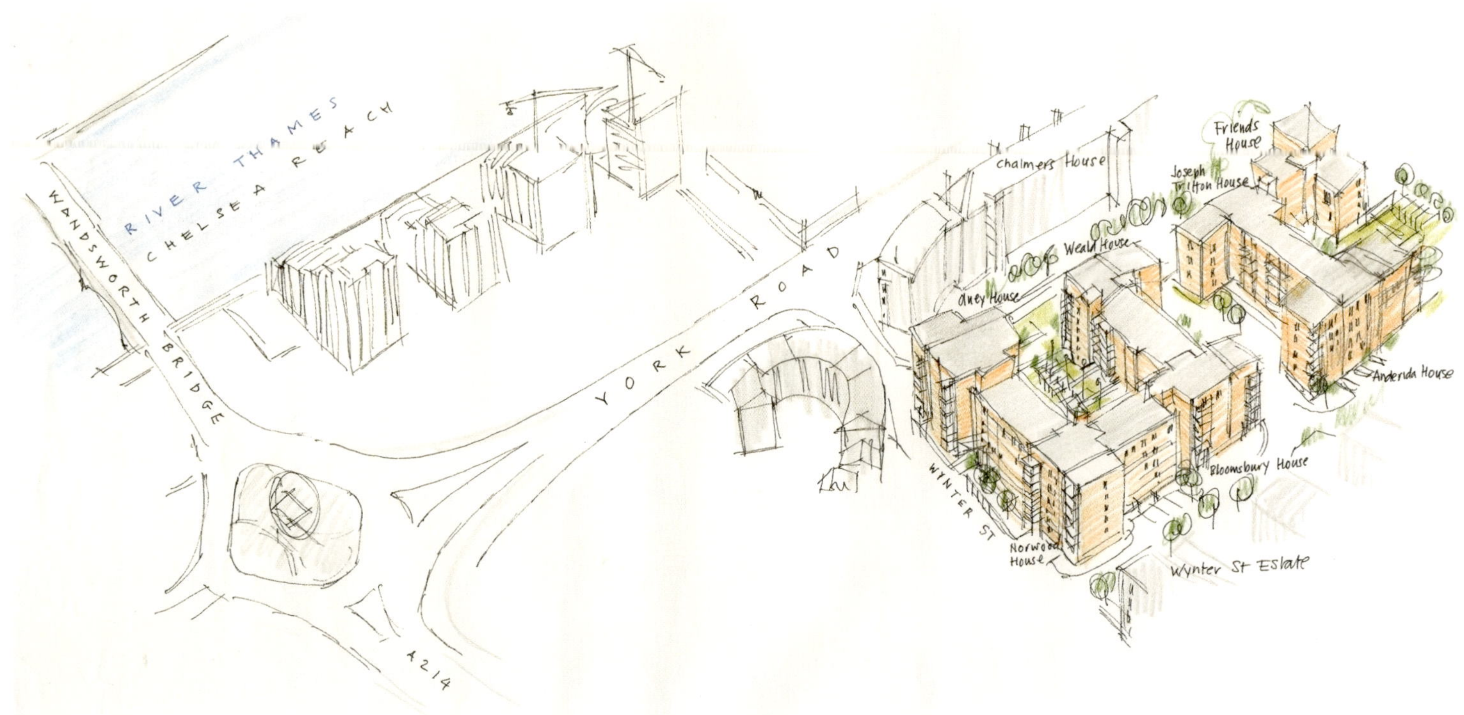

Opposite top: The former school site prior to redevelopment.
Opposite bottom: Joseph Tritton, Battersea.
Above: Layout plan for the Joseph Tritton site.
Bottom: Balcony detail at Joseph Tritton.

colourful wall tiles, are a key design feature that provide the building with aesthetics indistinguishable from nearby private residential developments. In common with the approach taken at the contemporaneously designed Pepys phase one, the entrances are marked by strong timber and glazing elements with clear elegant canopies.

The scheme was built using traditional construction methods, and the design palette and plans aimed to assimilate the development with the local area while providing the housing scheme with a distinct contemporary identity. Red brick and a selection of subtly different tones of stock brick was used throughout the development; layered in a contrasting combination of panels and stripes to create variation and character throughout the scheme. The brick layers were also highlighted with interspersed placement of lilac and turquoise ceramic tiles, applied behind the balconies and adjacent to the rear walkways.

Built to Housing Corporation Scheme Development Standards and Secured by Design principles, all the homes at Joseph Tritton were designed with generous space standards and are suitable for wheelchair visitors, while large windows ensure maximum lighting, without infringing on the privacy of neighbouring homes. All building materials were chosen for their low maintenance qualities, and the scheme as a whole is highly energy efficient, receiving an Eco-Homes rating of 'good'.

Reinforcing the link between the Joseph Tritton development and the unique attraction of the local area, including Battersea Park, the excellent rail and bus links to central London and the planned development of the Battersea Power Station, the scheme has been orientated to create new cycling routes and pedestrian thoroughfares that link with the local transport network. In keeping with the increasing emphasis on green space throughout the borough, a significant number of new trees were also added to the landscaping surrounding the development.

Opposite: Elevation of Joseph Tritton highlighting the brick frontage and the intended impact of the different coloured panelling.
Opposite bottom: The new Joseph Tritton site with mature landscaping.
Above: Ground floor site plan, illustrating the open plan living areas and separate kitchens.
Right: Galvanised steel and glass balconies add definition to the corner axis of the scheme.

River Mill Park

River Mill Park is a major regeneration project forming part of Lewisham's Urban Renaissance Scheme, and provides 211 mixed-tenure new homes on the former Sundermead Estate in Lewisham, South London. The £18 million project was completed in August 2007 and has succeeded in its aim of transforming what was once the site of a deteriorating Estate into a vibrant new place to live, offering traditional terraced houses with gardens and spacious apartments with balconies.

Having been initially engaged with the planned regeneration of the Estate as part of a masterplanning process with the London Borough of Lewisham, following a successful consultation and informed ballot process bptw were then contracted as lead designers to deliver the new residential community for London & Quadrant Housing Trust and Tower Homes.

Providing a diverse range of challenges in addition to the decant and demolition of the former 1960s buildings of the current Estate, the regeneration of Sundermead also involved the development of a redundant and contaminated depot situated adjacent to the Estate, and the naturalisation of the previously canalised River

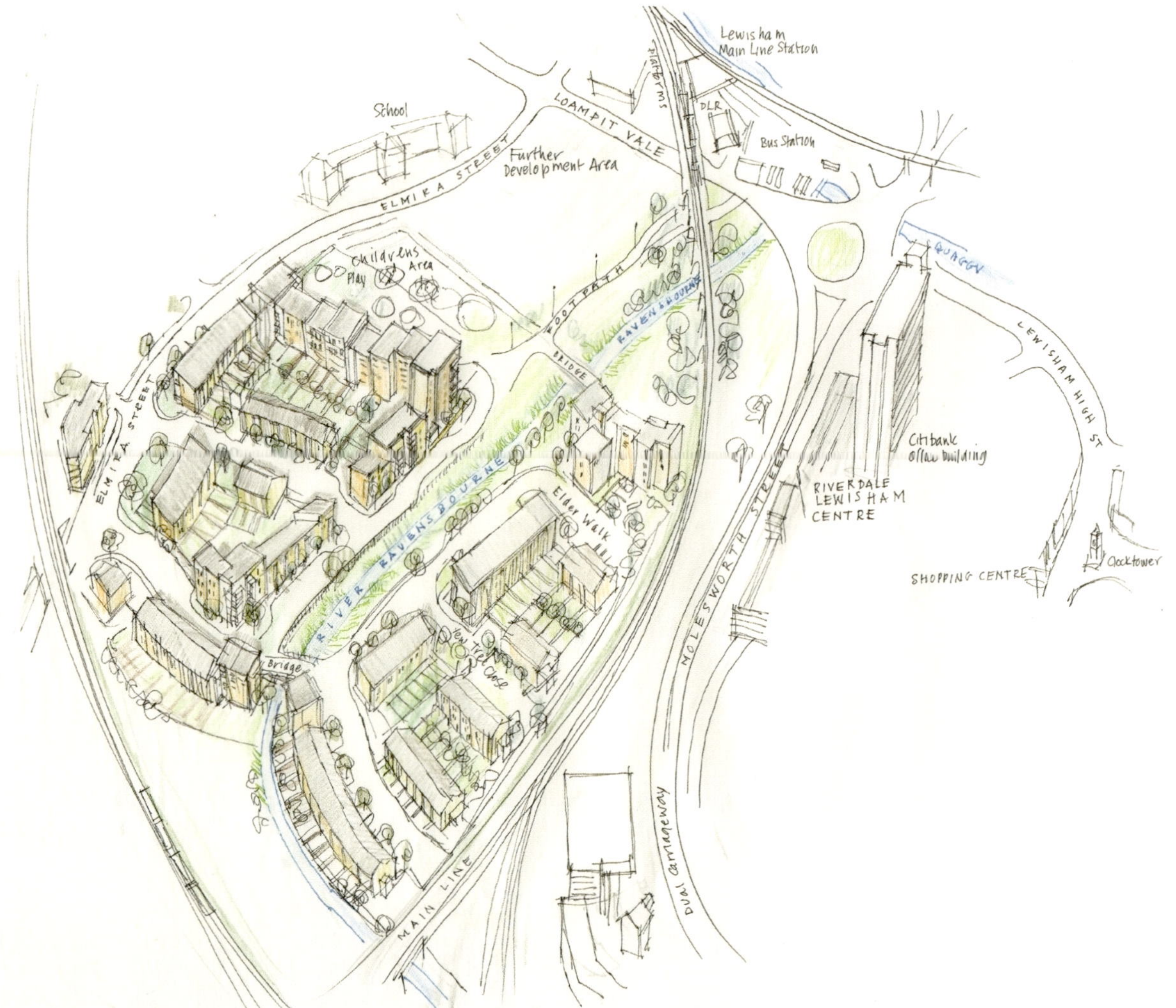

Left: River Mill Park, Lewisham.
Opposite top left: Aerial sketch of the proposed site layout.
Opposite bottom left: Model showing redevelopment option, a number of which were considered.
Opposite right: Site plan for River Mill Park incorporating the layout of the separate housing phases, the speed restriction tables (highlighted in pink) and the proposed SRB funded parkland to the north of the site.

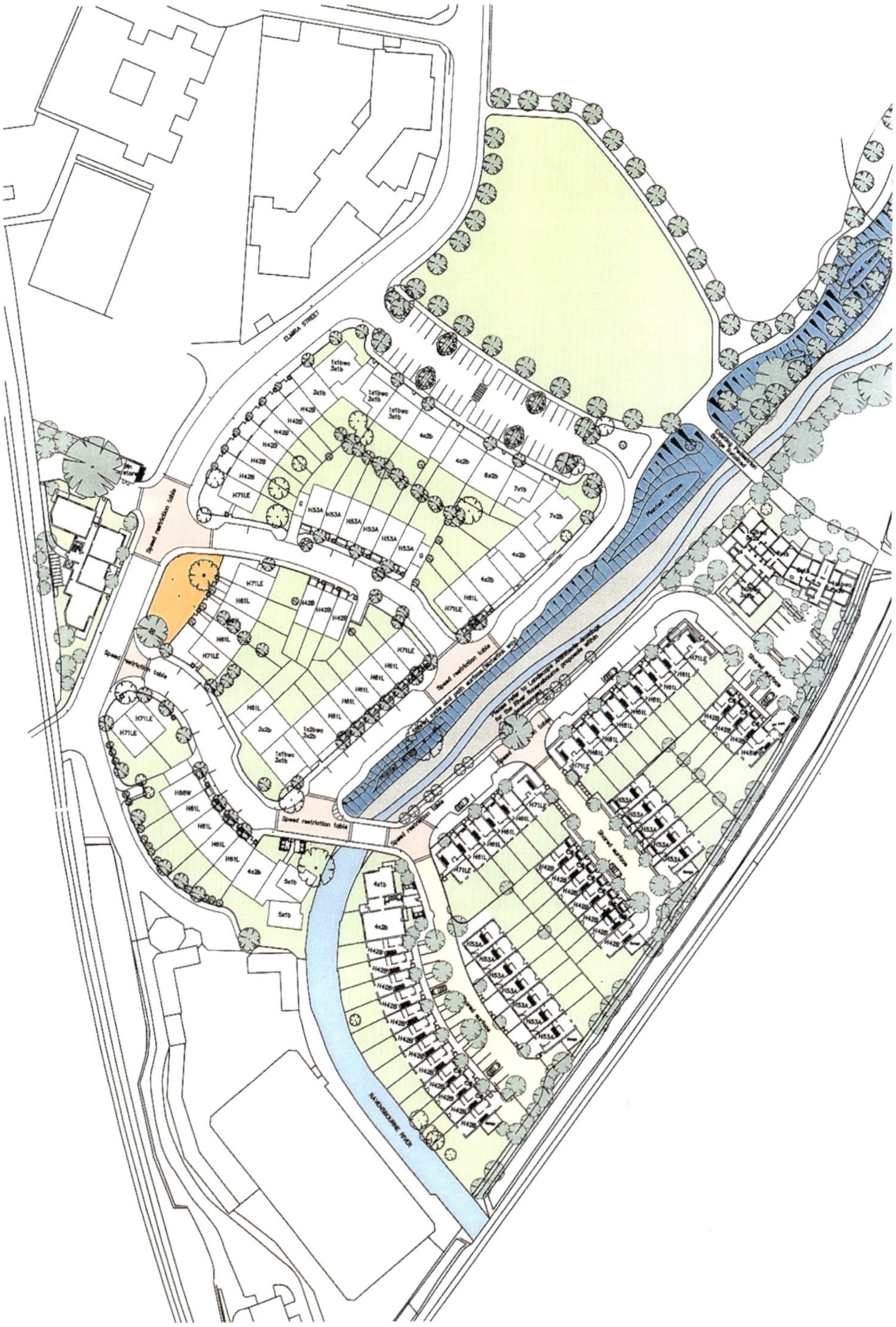

ELMIRA STREET
LOAMPIT VALE

Ravensbourne running throughout the centre of the site. Reconciling each of these factors to provide over 200 new affordable homes and Watermill Court, an assisted self-build project on the same site, the final masterplan also sought to connect the streetscape and layout of the River Mill Park development to nearby Lewisham town centre, railway station, pedestrian links over the river and newly created cycle paths.

Exploiting the location of the adjoining depot, the project was undertaken as a phased redevelopment programme; the former depot site developed in 2005 as the first phase, enabling residents to move from existing to new homes in a single transfer; and the second phase subsequently developed when existing homes had been vacated and demolished, eventually completed in 2007. In consideration of the extensive level of resident cooperation inevitably required throughout the decant and demolition process, the project involved high levels of community consultation from the onset and, working closely with London & Quadrant Housing Trust, Tower Homes, the London Borough of Lewisham and contractors, John Laing Partnership, the residents were involved from feasibility stage, through early strategic stages to final design proposals, attending exhibitions, designs workshops, consultation meetings and steering groups. All those who expressed a desire to stay locally were able to move into new homes in River Mill Park and

Top left and right: The Sundermead Estate, prior to the decant and demolition of the original 1960s buildings.
Bottom: The canalised River Ravensbourne, before its remodelling and naturalisation.
Opposite: Drawing from traditional Victorian neighbourhoods, terraces incorporated features such as stone paving, shorter curved streets and decorative ironwork.

had a considerable input into the final design details of the scheme, assisting in the selection of materials and finishes and naming of streets within the completed project.

Further extensive consultation was undertaken with key stakeholders, in particular the Environment Agency and Planning Officers, who held a critical role in the remodelling and naturalisation of the River Ravensbourne, and the redistribution of Metropolitan Open Land across the River Mill Park site, to provide a landscaped waterway, wider expanses of open space and play parks for the use of residents and a natural habitat for native species and plants.

The river frontage also provides one of the unique features of the River Mill Park homes, which range in size from one bedroom flats to four bedroom houses, with five homes fully accessible for wheelchair users. They comprise of a range of housing types including houses arranged in terraces with private gardens, and medium-rise apartments with private balconies which exploit River Mill Park's unique character as an urban development overlooking surrounding green space.

While accommodating a varying range of life-style needs, the scheme is also fully mixed-tenure; providing an even mix of homes for affordable rent and shared ownership, mirroring local housing needs and promoting sustainable

Top: After remodelling and naturalisation, the river became a popular natural resource and a focal point of the new neighbourhood.
Bottom left: Hand-drawn concept sketch of the River Ravensbourne and overlooking apartments.
Opposite: Elevation showing stepped apartment blocks of between six and eight storeys at the highest point.

patterns of development while helping to create a balanced community. Reflecting and supporting this balance the scheme is entirely tenure-blind, promoting the full integration of different groups and providing valuable cross-subsidy input to the scheme.

Underpinning the objective to achieve a clearly recognisable high quality end product, all homes have been designed and built to Lifetime Homes and Housing Corporation Scheme Development Standards, and are also compliant with the Wheelchair Housing Design Guide. In addition to generous space standards applied throughout the scheme, the designs for the houses include 'room in the roof' access to add value to the properties, the additional space made available as an easily accessible loft. Further supplementing the amount of private space available throughout the new neighbourhood, each of the houses were designed to include a back garden and front courtyard which accommodates refuse and bicycle storage.

Achieving a 'very good' Eco-Homes rating, all buildings have high thermal efficiency and the houses are fitted with central thermostat controlled gas fired 'wet' underfloor heating, reducing fuel costs. Preventing the homes from the noise of the adjacent railway, acoustic ventilators were added to all habitable rooms, predominantly to houses in phase one, in addition to the use of standard double glazing throughout the development and robust concrete frame construction.

Prefabricated bathroom pods were also used to minimise on-site trades to flatted buildings while thin joint Jamera concrete blocks were used for houses, largely only in the first phase of the development.

Maximising solar gain across the development, natural light was optimised through the use of internal windows in communal hallways and through the arrangement of dual aspect apartment blocks arranged in short streets and mews which, drawing on Georgian proportions of design, assimilates River Mill Park's scale and density with the architectural context of the surrounding area. Paved streets similarly emulate the pattern of a traditional inner-city residential neighbourhood while a strong identity for the scheme has been created through the mixed-use of red and buff bricks, interspersed with cream render and galvanised steel and timber balconies.

Incorporating home-zone principals, which feature significantly in the design of River Mill Park, careful landscaping and seating has also been integrated into the surroundings, offering residents and local people a place to sit, relax and enjoy the setting, while alternative elements incorporated into the design have the aim of encouraging reductions in vehicular speeds and creating a safer environment for pedestrians and cyclists. Featuring reduced road widths, short curving streets and cul-de-sacs; speed tables, chicanes and tree planting are also used to reduce the priority of the car, allowing residents to make their way through River Mill Park using safe, accessible thoroughfares connecting them to the nearby town centre and transport links.

Linking the physical regeneration of the former Sundermead Estate with the wider regeneration of the Lewisham area and the provision of new skills and opportunities for the local residents, the completion of River Mill Park also marked the achievement of the housing association's first self-build project in the South-East Thames region.

The shell of Watermill Court, which formed part of the first phase of River Mill Park's redevelopment, was initially designed by bptw and built by John Laing Partnership to link the external structure and aesthetics to the rest of the community. The self-build residents who had undergone a six week intensive training course were subsequently able to complete the internal work on their homes, carrying out basic construction, carpentry, painting and decorating. In tandem with the overall development, the residents of Watermill Court have access to a shared and separately enclosed garden, with the upper floor apartments benefiting from generous roof terrace balconies.

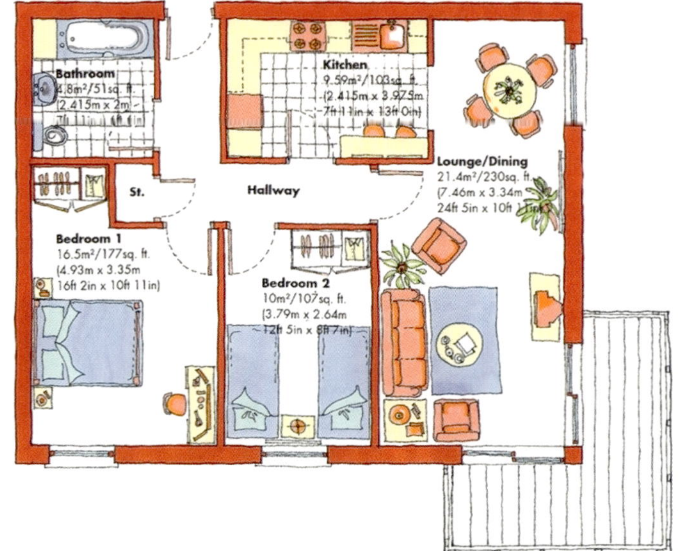

Opposite: Plan for a dual aspect two bedroom apartment illustrating corner balcony and windows for each bedroom in addition to the lounge area.
Top: The soft surface children's playground; a popular and well-used addition to the new, community-focussed landscape.
Bottom: All homes were built to Scheme Development Standards and feature generously spaced rooms and passageways compliant with the Wheelchair Housing Design Guide.

Left: River Mill Park block overlooking the River Ravensbourne.
Opposite top: Street patterns made up through the mixed-use of red and buff bricks, cream render and galvanised steel and timber balconies.
Opposite bottom left: Residents of the former Sundermead estate had the option of moving into the new River Mill Park, and had input into the choice of finishing features for their individual houses.
Opposite bottom right: The incorporation of home-zone principles, including wide, landscaped pavements and tree planting, served to create a pedestrian-orientated and resident-friendly streetscape.

Adapting for the Future

An appropriate reflection on two decades in practice and a contemporaneous period of significant development, January 2008 marked the advent of two important events in the practice's private and public calendar.

The first, bptw's twentieth year anniversary party, involved the gathering of every member of the practice and personal guests for a formal dinner and reception in London's Festival Hall. The occasion was a buoyant celebration of the working philosophy bptw partnership had cultivated and sustained throughout their two decades in practice.

While the practice had statistically transformed beyond recognition; its scope of work, and staff team continually expanding in volume and range, the practice's integrity and expertise in community consultation and people-focussed solutions remained integrally unchanged. Despite such significant expansion, the ratio of architectural partners to more junior staff has been maintained by senior appointments that crucially allow for the day-to day input of the highest quality technical knowledge and project guidance, and internally, the perpetuation of an egalitarian and mutually respectful working environment inclusive of all members of the practice.

Shortly following the anniversary celebration, Alan Wright's delivery of a keynote speech at the 2008 Housing Design Conference was the succeeding occasion of note, and a public marker of the respect the practice had gained through its steadfast provision of high quality, functional building solutions in the often under-celebrated social housing sector.

Under the overarching conference title, *Discovering, Designing and Delivering High Quality Homes*, bptw were, significantly, invited to address the concept of the Eco-town in relation to the future of house building and the development of sustainable communities. Reflecting bptw's increasing involvement in the debate surrounding urban sustainability and the recognition of the practice's application of practical environmental solutions within their own housing designs; it was also a discernible indicator of the inextricable association between the concept of sustainable development, and its role as a solution to the desperate shortage of UK affordable housing.

However, housing, in the broadest sense had dominated the national economic and social agenda since Gordon Brown's succession to the Labour premiership. Moving beyond John Prescott's ostensibly ambitious Communities Plan and the increased Housing Corporation Funding of the early millennium, the new Prime Minister launched his campaign with the declared aim to create a "home-owning, asset-owning, wealth-owning democracy"; the outcome of which would see a target-driven vision for housing that promised a new, easily accessible property ladder and a revived commitment to the provision of social housing. Including pledges to build three million new homes by 2020, an increase of 250,000 on any previous plan, and a 50 per cent overall rise in the social housing budget, it was inevitable that the implementation of this manifesto would have a significant, and immediate impact.

Visualisation for the Greenwich Wharf development in the context of the original Harbour Master's house adjacent to the scheme.

Befitting bptw who, subsequent to their work on Peckham Partnership had already proven their capacity to deliver large scale housing projects within challenging financial confines, the pressure on the housing sector to meet these development targets would manifest itself in the practice's appointment on a number of prominent high density, mixed-use and multi-tenured schemes; in London, further afield, and on the appositely local Greenwich Wharf development.

Following a masterplan for the transformation of 12 hectares of brownfield land into a development of 667 homes and mixed-use facilities, 2007 saw bptw partnership appointed by London & Regional Properties to design the 267 unit affordable housing component, of the East Greenwich scheme, masterplanned by Squire and Partners. A catalyst for design excellence and a critical link between East Greenwich and the town centre, parks and surrounding transport connections, the development held a particular significance for bptw; not only as a result of its local proximity but for the possibilities it allowed in terms of the renewable energy features it was able to incorporate. Designed to provide community heating linked to ground source heat pumps, and ultimately seeking to achieve an Eco-Homes rating of excellent, Greenwich Wharf was bptw's first large, sustainability-focussed project and afforded the practice an invaluable learning curve in their experience of adapting the architectural form to accommodate economically efficient renewable-energy features.

Underlining the increasing prevalence of schemes of this scale, bptw were concurrently appointed to implement the affordable housing design of over 370 homes as part of the £38 million transformation of the Chelsea Power Station in South-West London. Based on a masterplan by Terry Farrell & Partners with an objective to unify the two sides of the Lots Road site which straddled the boundaries of the Royal Borough of Kensington and Chelsea and the London Borough of Hammersmith and Fulham, the redevelopment aspires to create a 'new village'; eventually providing over 800 homes and mixed-use space.

In the context of its regeneration of a former industrial works, the scheme also bears similarities with Larden Road which, led by Logic Homes' founding partner Genesis Housing Group, was the largest, and most ambitious in bptw's experience of new build regeneration projects. In close collaboration with other Logic partners, bptw had been appointed to this scheme in the latter part of 2005 with a brief to provide a revised design solution for the high density, mixed-use development of the former Prestolite factory in the London Borough of Hammersmith and Fulham.

Despite the scheme having gained an initial planning permission prior to Genesis' involvement, significant and complex changes were required to overcome the challenges surrounding the orientation, accessibility, and density of the development; issues that due to the size and prominence of the scheme invoked direct scrutiny from the Mayor of London's office. Final permission realised, the project started on-site in 2007. The project retains the best of the original factory buildings and will eventually provide over 450 new homes for private and shared ownership and affordable rent in addition to significant commercial space and an extensive range of mixed-use amenities, including healthcare and employment space, public open space and play areas.

Opposite top: Larden Road, showing the central amenity space and cafe which is designed with full-height glazing to differentiate from the flats above. *Opposite bottom left and right*: 3-D concept models of Lots Road, showing the southwest aspect and aerial view.

Although ostensibly representative of a step-change in the range and focus of bptw partnership's work, the strategies involved in the creation of high density new-build developments, and the affordable housing component of such schemes in particular, notably required the same level of community understanding and the equivalent focus on the end user as bptw's earlier estate regeneration and refurbishment projects,

Using the same principles, but slightly revised methodologies such as, for instance, the analysis of feedback from residents of already completed new-build schemes, the practice continued to carry out widespread consultation and to involve local communities and neighbourhood groups in the design process, albeit without direct liaison with the literal existing or future residents of the greenfield sites. Thereby, irrespective of the change in development type, bptw's design process continued unchanged, to recognise and respond to the generic needs of the potential end user, within the unique context of the specific community the scheme would eventually impact upon.

Remaining committed to the need to maintain the social and economic diversity of people and activities within a neighbourhood, the refreshed popularity of mixed-use developments, and live-work schemes in particular, also enabled bptw to highlight the community revitalisation that could be achieved through a successful mixed-use local economy.

Illustrating this, recent bptw projects include Leven Road in Poplar; a new 60 home development incorporating the provision of 21 artist studios; Childers Street, designed to transform a disused industrial site in Deptford into shared-ownership apartments and community enterprise space; and Clyde Terrace, a mixed-use scheme in Forest Hill which has commercial units for the flexible use of local businesses, in addition to a residential component of ten affordable live-work homes.

Respectively developed for Swan, Circle Anglia and London & Quadrant Housing Associations, all were relatively new ventures for the social housing sector. Reflecting this, all three projects were similarly concerned with the need for the mixed-use amenities to meet the requirements of the existing and future residents of the sites. Reflecting Jane Jacobs' prescription for the urban community and her emphasis on the need for social and economic neighbourhood interaction; through accessible amenities, local industriousness and communal areas conducive to physical interaction, the urban realm remained the chief focus of each project. Inclusive of the streetscape and pedestrian accessibility to local transport links, bptw thereby continue to underline the significance of the active street frontage; the relationship between its commercial and residential function and the need for high quality urban living to be founded in the proximity of individuals and families to work and recreation space, in addition to the services required for everyday life.

Heightened by the increased demand for more complex mixed-use schemes, and compounded in part, by general concern over the commercial drivers of the sector and the implications of ill-advised decision-making, accurate and timely planning procedure subsequently became increasingly important to the delivery of urban design schemes and large scale development. Directly responding to this, bptw introduced an additional discipline to the practice; led by Mark Gibney, and launched in September 2007, the new planning service not only attracted new clients to bptw, but provided the other disciplines within the practice with an invaluable source of private and public sector advice on planning issues, strategies and the environmental impact of design.

Opposite top: Final visualisation of Leven Road showing the view of the project from the easterly aspect.
Opposite bottom left: View of the completed Clyde Terrace showing the upper level residential units and ground floor commercial space.
Opposite bottom right: Visualisation of Childers Street highlighting the main street frontage.

Similarly responding to changes in the industry and specifically, to the exponential rate of growth in software and clients' increasingly high expectations of technical efficiency and visual output, since 2004, visualisation had also gained momentum as one of bptw's core disciplines. Expanding on its role as an exclusively internal service the team became a highly reputable arm of the practice offering external clients a range of multi-media and graphic design solutions for work in its own right under the leadership of partner, Mark Waite. Achieving new levels of recognition for their service, April 2008 saw the visualisation team's animation work featuring in the National Science Museum's sustainability-focussed Science of Survival exhibition, which, since receiving significant acclaim in the UK, has subsequently embarked on a global tour.

Despite its growing client base, the visualisation team and the services it provides remain indispensable to bptw's internal working. Building on the practice's longstanding use of physical models and computer generated 3-D massing reproductions of design ideas, the provision of two- and three-dimensional photorealistic imaging and animated walk-through presentations represented the future stage of communication with clients, developers and even residents who were able to use the visualisations to contextualise and interact with the designs in progress.

More broadly, the practice's continual review of their internal structure and services and its overall willingness to affect change at the most fundamental level, was a significant marker of the way in which bptw's partners and, to a large extent, the associate and staff-led business planning teams envisaged the future of the practice. However, while indicating their dedication to continued quality and a culture of forward thinking development, bptw's preparedness to adapt their multi-disciplinary approach, according to sector-specific, political, economic and social change, was notably, just the most visible tip of an extensive underlying commitment to research and development involving every level of the practice.

Exemplifying this, staff development remained a foremost priority and the appointment of Carol Strevens, head of finance and human resources, as partner in 2006 also reinforced the practice's commitment to each of the key aspects of the business, in addition to the firm priority given to internal progress. Allowing for the extensive exchange of knowledge, idea-sharing and inspiration between the practice's architectural teams, weekly design reviews held on projects continue to ensure practice-wide familiarity with all active schemes and the opportunity for projects to receive the maximum amount of design input from staff of every level of seniority.

Technologically, the practice has also developed a web-based document management portal, specific to bptw, which is now a pioneering knowledge-sharing system available to all staff. Additionally, bptw has also been recognised by the Royal Institute of British Architects for its established in-house CPD training programme; a series of fortnightly seminars co-ordinated entirely by staff, which continues to be noted as an exemplar model of successful staff development.

Underlining a similar investment in the external exchange of knowledge and development of best practice, and extending this comparison of contemporary innovation and development to an international setting, bptw also organised and participated in a number of tours to exemplary housing schemes in the UK and overseas. Among them, the 2007 Design for Homes sponsored tour of Stockholm's Hammarby Sjostad, a former brownfield site now internationally acclaimed as a leading sustainable urban development and pioneer of carbon-neutral living, would prove pivotal for bptw. Recognising their accordance with the social, environmental and technical design principles of the Hammarby masterplan, the practice later cultivated a relationship with Tengbomgruppen Architects who were involved in the design of the scheme. bptw subsequently invited the Swedish practice to speak at a seminar in London in October 2007 and a spirit of mutual collaboration was established that would support both practices' pursuit of integrated design solutions for urban sustainability.

Erring away from the design of environmentally exemplary but isolated housing in favour of more encompassing efficient and smart solutions for transport, energy and cohesive community living, bptw's distinctively holistic approach to sustainability would serve to characterise the practice's response to the ever-increasing pressure on the housing industry to work to the government's extensive environmental targets. Including pledges for all new homes to be carbon neutral by 2016, stringent regulations for housing developers to comply with the Code for Sustainable Homes, a guide across all sustainability issues launched in 2006; and in the London Renewables Toolkit, a promise to generate 10 per cent of UK electricity from renewable sources by 2010, these would, nevertheless have an immediate impact on bptw's approach to housing design.

The success of the Logic Homes consortia projects in meeting and surpassing these regulations was a considerable reflection on both the increasing effectiveness of this important partnership, the very success of whose integrated supply chain relied upon the versatility of its multi-disciplinary approach and collaboration with its partners, and bptw's capacity for future expansion; in terms of the geographical location of the practice's schemes, the nature of the homes within those developments, and specifically, the practice's propensity to accept the new challenges of sustainable design in correlation with the increasing need for viable family housing within an urban setting.

Epitomising this, the thermal insulation and noise reduction properties of the timber frame technology of Logic Homes' Cranes Farm Road in Basildon, gained the scheme a 'very good' rating by Eco-Home Standards, while the development overall, comprising of 48 mixed-tenure houses and 12 flats for affordable rent, was almost catalytic in its approach to community design, with an emphasis on the principles of the home-zone, a focus on pedestrian over vehicular safety, and layout and landscaping design conducive to a child-friendly environment.

Extending this further, Great Billing Way, another Challenge Fund II project designed and masterplanned by bptw for Genesis, incorporates an extensive range of community and family-focussed home-zone concept landscape and design features. The greenfield site development in Northampton providing 126 family houses and 36 flats, also includes the wide use of solar hot water technology, and various rain water attenuation measures.

Similarly incorporating renewable energy features into a wide range of additional projects, such as the ground source heating system integrated into the plans for Greenwich Wharf and various energy saving measures incorporated into Larden Road, including wind turbines, community heating technology and bio-fuel boilers, bptw experienced little difficulty in designing to the new standards.

Opposite top: Animations produced by bptw visualisation team for the National Science Museum's Science of Survival exhibition
Opposite bottom: Sketch of Great Billing Way, showing the prominent green landscaping and home-zone design features
Above: View of the completed Cranes Farm Road, showing a row of terraced family homes.

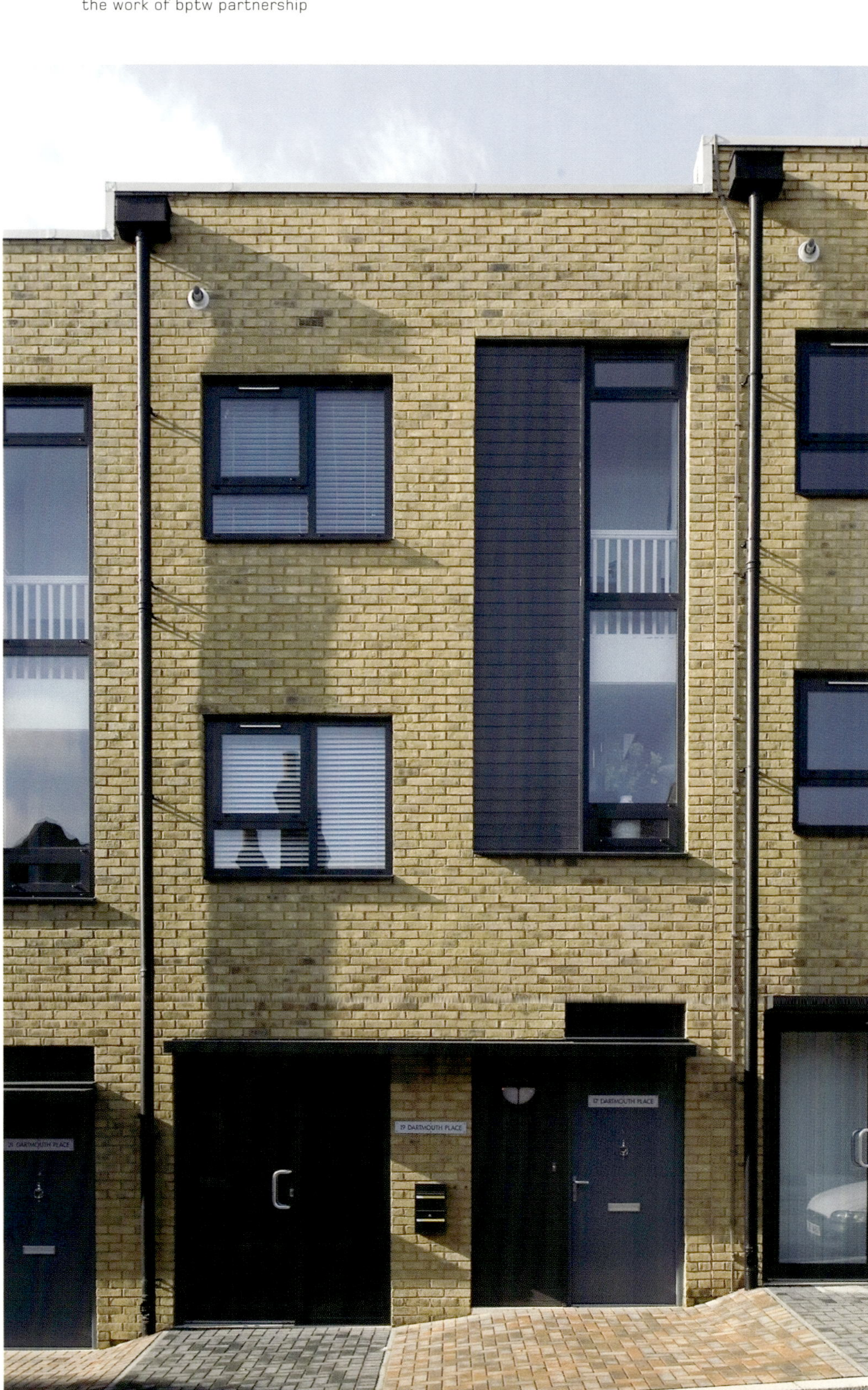

Main facade of live-work homes in part of the Clyde Terrace development.

However, within the practice, underlying concern remained over the relative superficiality of designing to target percentages and over the industry's visible tendency to incorporate recognisable eco-gadgetry without greater attention to the basic fabric and integrity of the building envelope.

Avoiding this predilection, bptw's focus remained on the wider development of sustainable communities, and the interactive systems of living, working and playing that encompassed 'green architecture' as part of the overall urban environment. Simultaneously, instead of rigidly following the guidelines for stringent carbon-neutral housing developments, the practice's design teams consciously aspired to the development of passively serviced homes; those so well constructed, air tight and designed according to principles of strategic orientation, light capture and robust design, that they can be maintained with minimal energy requirements.

While bptw's projects were still predominantly London-based, their steady but critical expansion into Essex, Northampton and further afield, Greater Manchester, where they gained considerable acclaim for their masterplan and regeneration work on the Ordsall Estate, spoke volumes of the practice's ability to apply their legacy of contextual, responsive design to the idiosyncrasies of individual communities, irrespective of geographical location, or socio-economic background.

Maintaining, above all, that architecture, particularly in the social sector, should endeavour to satisfy the aesthetic taste and functional requirements of the resident, as the end user, above the favour of their professional contemporaries, bptw therefore continue to pride themselves on their delivery of successful, imaginative and responsible projects that will remain at the forefront of high quality housing design for decades to come.

Drawing on 20 years of practice experience, the lessons learnt from extensive first-hand consultation and the precedents set by their architectural contemporaries, bptw continues to approach each project as a process of growth; refusing to take an academic checklist approach to urban regeneration or development but adapting instead, their own comprehension of its design and constraints according to the response of the community it is due to serve.

Clyde Terrace

A forward thinking scheme situated within a conservation area in Forest Hill in the London Borough of Lewisham, the Clyde Terrace mixed-use development has transformed a vacant industrial building, previously used for manufacturing purposes, to provide new residential and commercial space ideally located for transport links from Forest Hill railway station.

Appointed to deliver the £7.5 million scheme for London & Quadrant Housing Group, bptw worked in partnership with building contractors, Allenbuild, and employers agent EC Harris, to develop Clyde Terrace as one of many new projects undertaken as part of the Forest Hill Urban Design Framework and the extensive regeneration of the local area.

Approaching the design of Clyde Terrace in the context of this wider redevelopment process, bptw supported their planning application for the scheme with the provision of what was essentially a masterplan for the overall improvement of the area between Forest Hill's high street and the land running alongside the railway edge. Including proposals, later endorsed by the Local Authority, for the use of sites adjacent to Clyde Terrace, bptw subsequently adopted an instrumental role in the wider transformation of the area and the consortia's project became an integral part of the whole scheme.

Completed in 2008, Clyde Terrace's highly visible structure comprises of two buildings and accommodates a total of 52 new homes, including 30 for rent, 12 for shared ownership and ten live-work units. Six commercial units were allocated to the ground floor of the scheme and the size, layout and design of each unit varies in order to provide flexible options for the adaptation of local businesses. Directly responding to the London Borough

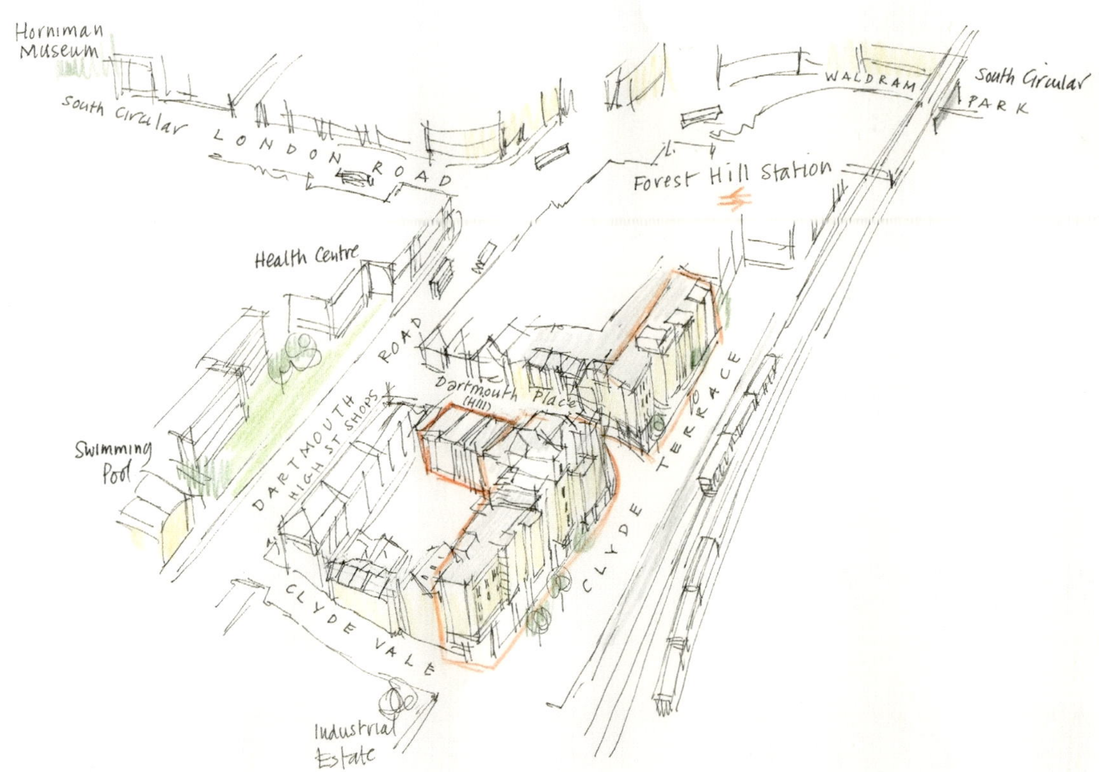

Left: Clyde Terrace, Forest Hill.
Opposite: View of the completed Clyde Terrace showing the upper level residential units and ground floor commercial space.

PW
Printworks
020 8663 4466

of Lewisham's objective to provide businesses and homes which would add vigour to the social and economic framework of the local community, there is potential for approximately 80 new jobs to be created as a result of the Clyde Terrace development, while the appeal of new, affordable homes directly beside a station linked to key central London interchanges has significant attraction for new commuters to the area.

Significant for its role in heightening the commercial and residential appeal of the area, Clyde Terrace is juxtaposed between the commercial frontage of the high street to the west and the adjacent railway to the east. A significant physical determinant in the scheme's design, the change in gradient between the two borders fundamentally manifests itself in the increase in scale to six storeys in response to the frontage of the railway line.

In addition to the varying changes in level, the need to connect Clyde Terrace's new community, the existing residential and commercial properties and the railway station, also impacted on the planning for the orientation of the building and the circulation and layout of public thoroughfares. Reinforcing the railway as an environmentally friendly and easily accessible travel option, bptw's overall masterplan was informed by the desire to create routes for safe pedestrian use, with designs for Clyde Terrace incorporating the careful reshaping of the surrounding urban context.

Most notably, bptw partnership's design impacted on the main thoroughfare from the high street to the railway station. Whereas direct access was previously blocked by the monolithic state of the former industrial building, forcing pedestrians along an enclosed narrow alleyway flanked by the edge of the manufacturing unit, bptw created a more secure, clearly orientated pathway through the centre of Clyde Terrace which is lined with glass fronted commercial units. Providing a continuous active frontage, the pathway also increases passive surveillance within the area and heightens the natural interchange between residents, commercial traders and pedestrians making use of the thoroughfare. Similarly contributing to the increased security and transparency of the thoroughfare and the public realm overall, the pathway is also protected and overlooked by the residents' of Clyde Terrace's overlooking properties.

Complementing the transparent frontage of the commercial units, apartments on each floor of Clyde Terrace are arranged around fully glazed stair cores that provide direct access to the street. Adding to openness of the building, properties on the upper levels also benefit from roof terrace balconies. The remaining exterior of the scheme features varying tones of brick and render cladding, offset by timber panels. Responding to the acoustic issues associated with the adjacent railway, the noise from which was potentially a significant issue for the residential properties, bptw designed a fully glazed enclosed sunspace or 'winter garden', which can be opened up in summer to act as a balcony or enclosed in winter to form a conservatory, into each living room facing the railway. A sustainable, efficient and cost-effective solution to the need to buffer the noise from the transport link, the sunspaces serve to maximise the views and solar gain of each apartment, extending the living space for the residents while reducing the need for expensive ventilation or triple glazing.

Left: Concept sketch of the scheme entrance and commercial space at ground floor level.
Opposite left: Apartment entrances, arranged around glazed stair cores providing communal access to the street.
Opposite top right: Contemporary landscaping mirrors the material and design of the scheme's architecture.
Opposite bottom right: View of Dartmouth Road looking towards the railway line.

Top: The striking angular entranceway on the corner of the development.
Bottom: Site plan of Clyde Terrace.
Opposite: Sunspaces provide additional living space and an acoustic buffer from the railway line opposite.

Cranes Farm Road, Basildon

Incorporating modern design with appealing landscaping and an innovative use of mixed-tenure units, Cranes Farm Road; an £8.5 million Logic Homes project for Genesis Housing Group delivered through English Partnerships and the Housing Corporation Challenge Fund II programme, was designed to address the need for improvements in Basildon's housing stock, while promoting confidence in the local perception of shared ownership and affordable housing.

Following instruction by Genesis Housing Group and working with contractors, Allenbuild, bptw partnership developed the masterplan and design for the scheme of 12 two bedroom flats and 48 family dwelling houses, ranging from two bedroom to four bedroom homes and mainly comprising of low-rise two storey buildings. Demonstrating a forward thinking approach to financially accessible housing, the 100 per cent affordable scheme provides an almost equal mix of homes for affordable rent and shared ownership. The development is entirely 'tenure blind', with the rented and part-owned homes indistinguishable from each other in terms of construction material and location within the site.

Rising to the challenges posed by the sharp, steep levels of the site, bptw focussed on developing Cranes Farm Road in conjunction with the neighbouring housing estate and the boundaries of the adjacent ecological wildlife area. The natural aspects of the land were used to take advantage of local views while also providing the opportunity for pitched roofscapes, stepped gardens and building layouts positioned to have as much south, west and east light as possible.

The scheme was handed over in seven stages and modern methods of construction were used throughout the delivery of the project. Timber frames, carefully selected from managed sources and manufactured off-site, were extensively used and contributed to the scheme's 'very good' rating by Eco-Homes standard. Integrated features such as the timber clad roof terraces and bay windows simultaneously allowed additional natural daylight to enter the homes, extending the internal living areas without overlooking other houses in the process. Adding to the scheme's sustainability credentials, bathroom pods were manufactured off-site and incorporated to help reduce the impact of on-site construction time.

Fulfilling the aspiration to nurture a sense of pride and ownership in all residents of Cranes Farm Road, it was ensured that public space was varied, useful, accessible and attractive. Combining light grey coloured paviours for pathways and natural riven paving for garden footpaths, different colours and varied textures to the roads and pavements are used as a subtle and appealing demarcation of changes of use and ownership. Drawing on concepts for pedestrian priority and the streetscapes and parking courts of developments such as the more traditionally based Poundbury and the more contemporary Abode in Harlow, the scheme arguably represents a catalyst for new ways of UK thinking towards a number of issues; particularly regarding the principals of the home-zone, the separation of vehicular and pedestrian areas and the endorsement of shared surfaces.

Opposite top: View of the townhouses, featuring elongated vertical timber window bays.
Opposite bottom: An aerial plan of the site, modelling the layout of houses, vehicular thoroughfares and gardens according to home-zone principles.
Above: Mixed hard and soft landscaping and different coloured paviours act as a visual indicator of the change between pedestrian and vehicular surface areas.
Right: Set into a green site, and bordering an ecological wildlife area Cranes Farm Road achieves a sense of space, openness and relative quiet while benefitting from the extensive nearby transport links.

Top: A double-fronted house, with four large bedrooms and private external space with gardens to the front and rear.
Bottom: Site plan of Cranes Farm Road.
Opposite: Semi-detached houses with large bay windows and timber cladding.
Opposite bottom: Material for the internal timber frame and integrated external features was selected from carefully managed sustainable sources.

Talbot Road, Northampton

Transforming a historic industrial site into an exemplary £4.7 million new-build housing scheme providing family homes in a key development area on the outskirts of Northampton, Talbot Road was delivered by the Logic Homes consortia with bptw as architects and Hill Partnership as contractor for Genesis Housing Group.

With the objective to provide a range of housing types for a mix of affordable tenure, bptw's designs for Talbot Road converted the former boot factory and adjoining printworks site into a development of 52 homes, providing a range of one and two bedroom accommodation for a mix of affordable rent and shared ownership options. Built to generous space standards throughout, five of the homes are adapted for mobility use and car parking has been made available for 87 per cent of the units directly under the footprint of the building. Responding to the slope of the Talbot Road site, half of the car park effectively forms a basement to the building. In addition, bptw also allowed for the provision of sufficient cycle storage facilities for the entire development.

Set between two local roads connected by a corridor running north to south through the development, the Talbot Road buildings have been arranged in a three-sided courtyard shaped block, open to the east facing aspect and varying in elevation with six storeys at the highest point. Strengthening the link between the two streets, full-height glazing and brick patterning have been used to create strong entrances and a vertical hierarchy that continues throughout the development, exemplified in the positioning of the windows and the ratio of clear to etched glazing used to provide daylight and privacy where needed. Heightening the sense of community and security among residents, the location of both entrances provide opportunity for natural surveillance; the front entrance primarily over the residential apartments, and the rear, over the enclosed play area and the point of vehicular and pedestrian access to the car park and general needs unit.

The materials used on the project are mainly brick, slate and laminate panels, but careful attention to the treatment of the brickwork has resulted in an effective textured look, consciously designed to reflect the historic industrial usage of the site in terms of the proportions of the window openings and the vertical and horizontal patterning around the doorways and cills. Deep coping at terrace level further balances the horizontal patterns with the vertical windows, creating greater embellishment at eaves level and where the setback Trespa occurs on the highest levels at the top floor. The use of colour throughout the building has been achieved through a combination of a small palette of materials to provide simple yet effective patterning and texture.

Using modern methods of construction, including Light Gauge Steel Frame to heighten the efficiency and cost-effectiveness of the delivery of Talbot Road, the new-build development was successfully completed in April 2008, just 18 months after work started on-site.

Above: View of the Talbot Road scheme from the park opposite.
Right: Front elevation of Talbot Road.

Greenwich Wharf

The culmination of two years of planning and constructive, collaborative working in partnership, the visionary Greenwich Wharf development started on-site in spring 2008 and is planned to be delivered in phases over the course of three years, ultimately transforming a large scale site, comprising of Lovell's, Granite, Badcock's and Pipers Wharves, on the western side of the Greenwich peninsula.

Following a masterplan for the transformation of 12 hectares of previously disused industrial land into a development of 667 mixed tenure homes and mixed-use facilities, 2007 saw bptw partnership appointed by London & Regional Properties to work in partnership with Squire & Partners as the leading design firm and masterplanner, to design the £43 million affordable housing component of the East Greenwich scheme and also 29 homes for private sale within the same apartment blocks.

With the affordable element comprising a total of 236 homes, 10 per cent of which were specifically designed for wheelchair use and 35 per cent for family housing, bptw provided the planning and detailed design for four blocks of apartments consisting of one, two and three bedroom flats, and four bedroom houses, ranging from three to seven storeys. The layouts of all the apartments and houses provide spacious living standards fulfilling Lifetime Homes and Scheme Development Standards. Consent for Greenwich Wharf was eventually achieved in November 2006 and will be delivered by a team including, in additional to the architectural partners, contractor Durkan Limited, planning consultant DP9, services

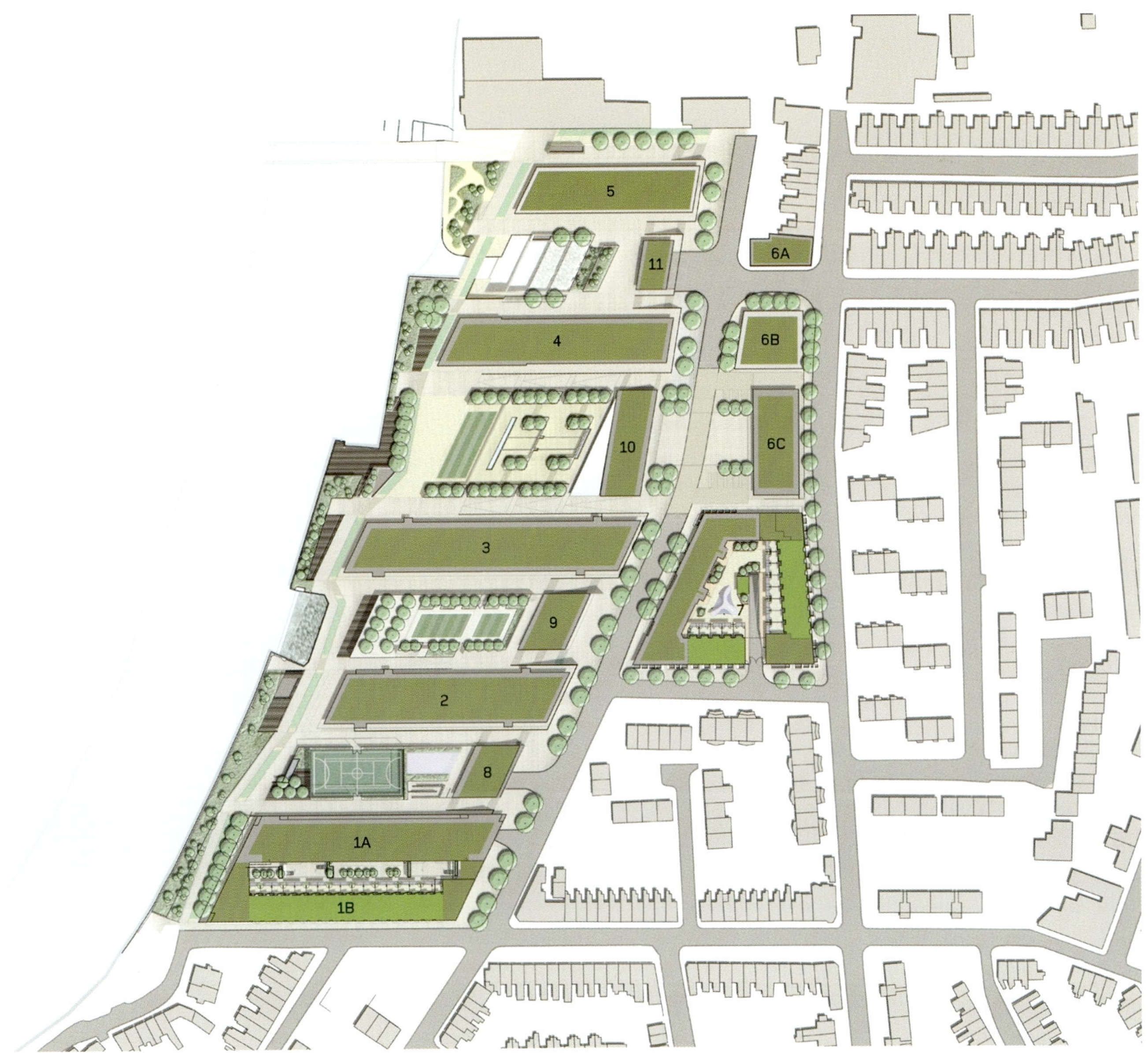

Opposite: Greenwich Wharf, Greenwich
Above: The overall Squire & Partners Greenwich Wharf masterplan showing the four wharves and proposed landscaping.
Overleaf: Visualisation of the Greenwich Wharf flats and landscaped courtyard area, showing the views overlooking the River Thames.

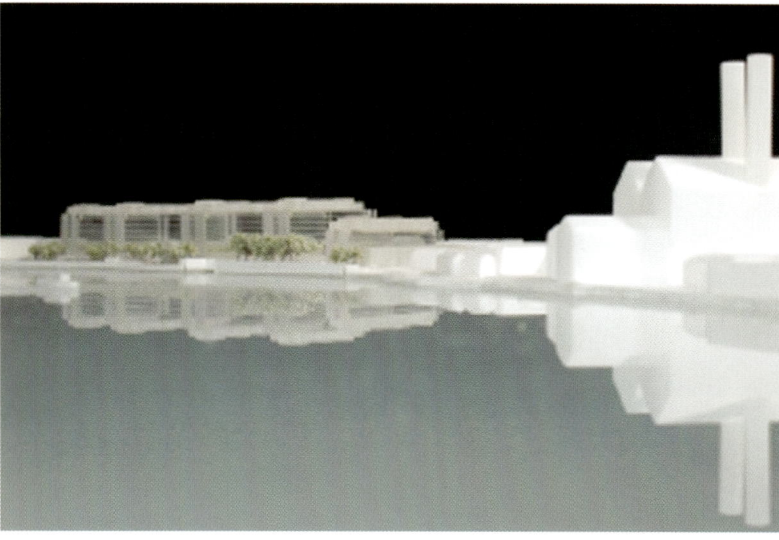

Above: 3-D concept plan of a three bedroom apartment, incorporating balcony space and a flexible living layout.
Bottom: A concept massing model illustrating the scheme's proximity to the River Thames and in context with the nearby power station.
Opposite: Side elevation of the development from the River Thames, illustrating the varying storey heights and the relationship between the scheme and the adjacent river bank.

engineer Blyth and Blyth, structural engineer Expedition Engineering, landscape architect Land Use Consultants and Tweeds as Quantity Surveyor and Employers Agent.

Aspiring to deliver the very best in sustainable design, bptw's design for Greenwich Wharf maximises the residential properties' potential for unique views over the River Thames whilst orienting spaces for optimum solar gain and temperature control. Additionally, the scheme is also set to achieve an Eco-Homes rating of 'excellent' for the houses and 'very good' for the apartments and incorporates a range of renewable energy strategies including a community heating system linked to ground source heat pumps for the provision of hot water and under floor heating systems, surface water attenuation tanks, green roofs on all houses and green/brown roofs on each of the flats.

Maximising the use of materials formerly found on the original Greenwich Wharf site, stock brick and render feature throughout the btpw's scheme, contrasting with the zinc and slate on neighbouring apartment blocks while assimilating the new development with the surrounding residential community in Greenwich; drawing on the mixed features of its many Victorian and Georgian houses and listed buildings.

Beyond this, the integration of local public space forms a crucial element of the scheme; one of the project's chief objectives being the linking of the East Greenwich community to the World Heritage listed sites of Maritime Greenwich. Particularly relevant to bptw's component of the development, the Thames Path weaves alongside the buildings designed by the practice and careful efforts have been made to incorporate the path as an integral part of the surrounding landscaping. On a wider scale, the planned addition of mixed-use elements to include retail and office space, sports facilities and hotel accommodation will also serve to connect Greenwich Wharf with the more commercially buoyant East Greenwich Peninsula, home to the newly transformed Millennium Dome, North Greenwich Underground station and the already established residential Greenwich Millennium Village.

Above: A final visualisation of Greenwich Wharf from the River Thames showing the scheme in context with the surrounding buildings.
Opposite: Three bedroom unit plan.

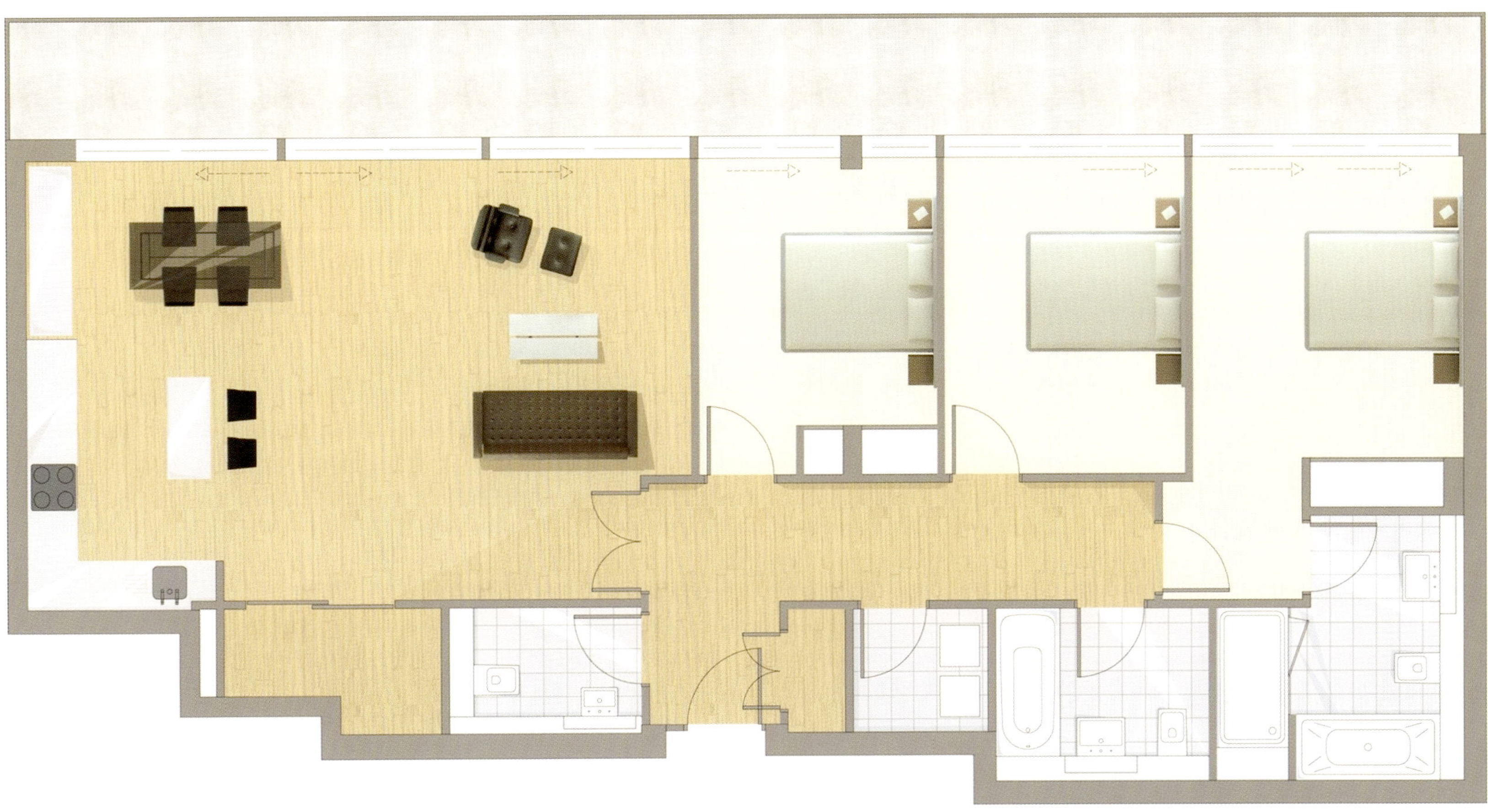

Larden Road

The largest and most ambitious in bptw's experience of new-build regeneration projects, bptw became involved with the development of Larden Road in the latter part of 2005. Despite the scheme having gained an initial planning permission, with a brief to provide a revised design solution for the high density, mixed-use development of the 2.4 hectare site of a former Prestolite factory in Shepherd's Bush, London Borough of Hammersmith and Fulham, there were significant challenges surrounding the orientation, accessibility, and density of the development before the £62 million project received final permission and started on-site in 2007.

Working closely with members of Logic Homes Partnership, who were appointed to work on Larden Road by housing association Genesis Housing Group, bptw, in conjunction with architects SHP, contractor Durkan Ltd, along with living architects and landscape architects Farrer Huxley Associates, developed an independent but co-ordinated design for specific areas of the scheme, linked to each of the other partnering architects' schemes through the overall landscape design.

Retaining the best of the original factory buildings, the project will eventually provide over 450 new homes of a

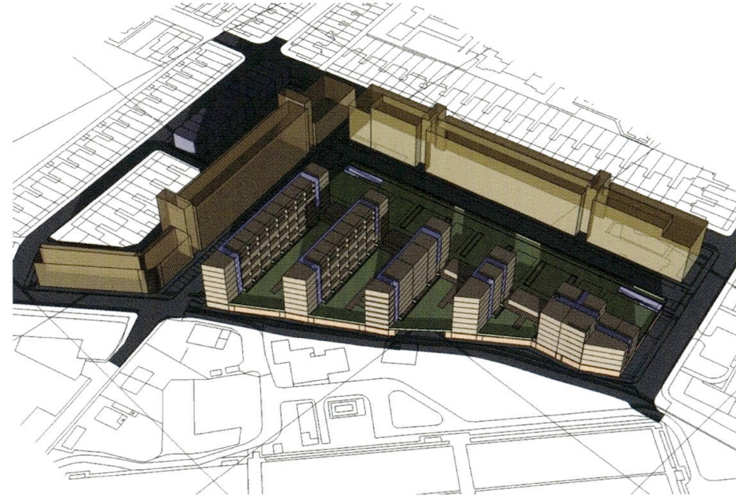

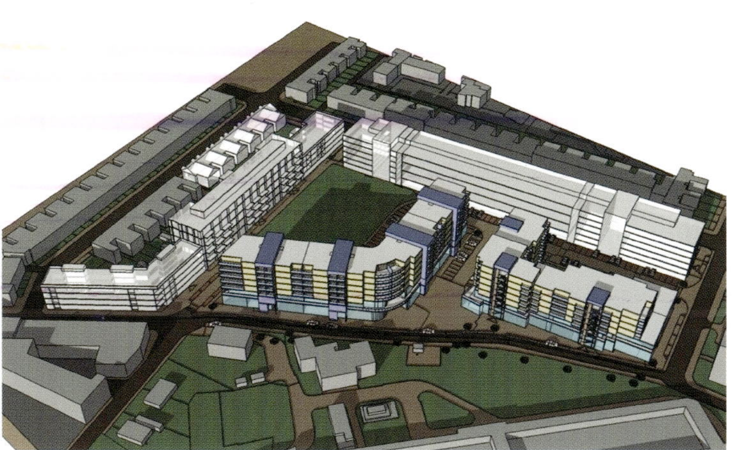

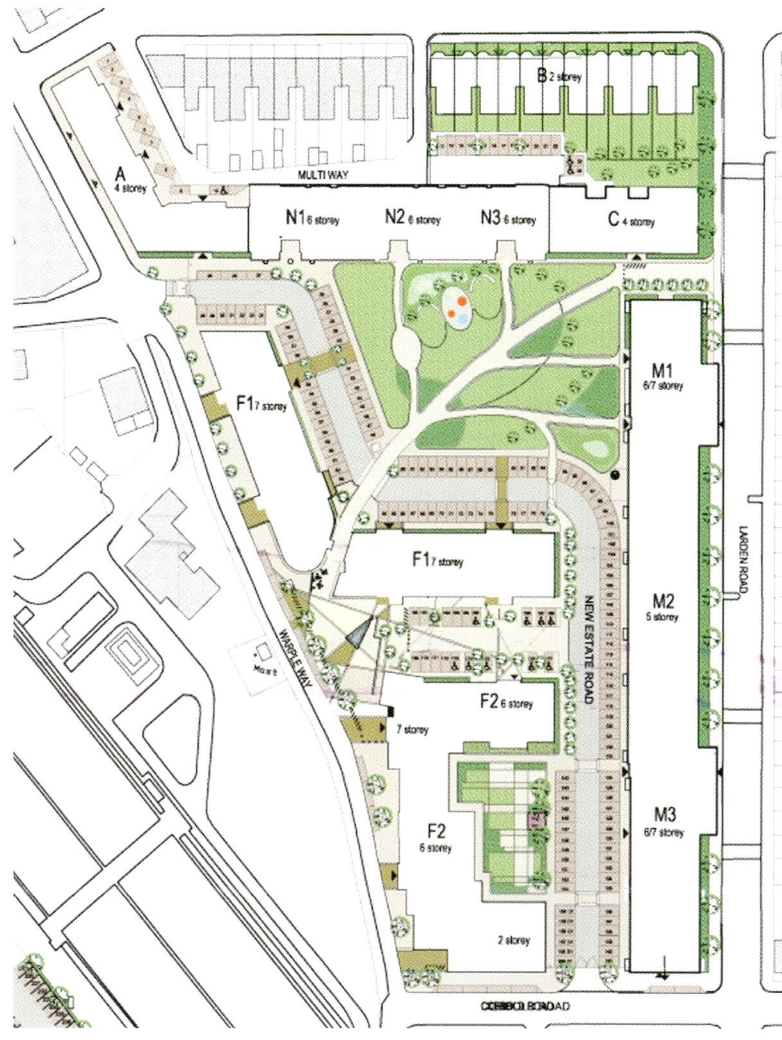

Opposite left top and bottom: View of the original site showing the former Presolite factory buildings.
Opposite right: Larden Road, Shepherd's Bush.
Top and bottom left: Models showing changes in the design of the scheme according to the results of the sunlight and daylight surveys; the orientation of the blocks were altered for the final scheme (top) after problems with density and light shortages were exposed in the original design proposals (bottom).
Right: Aerial plan of the full Larden Road site.

tenure mix comprising approximately 70 per cent private and shared ownership and 30 per cent affordable rent, in addition to 3,500 square metres of commercial space and approximately 100 square metres for an extensive range of mixed-use amenities including healthcare and education and community facilities, public open space and play areas. Almost 300 car parking spaces will also be provided, slightly over a third of which will be located off-site. Encouraging more environmentally friendly means of transport meanwhile, cycle links to the local community have been significantly enhanced and extensive bike storage space has been provided throughout the scheme.

Comfortably meeting the Greater London Authority's requirements for the provision of 10 per cent renewable energy, various sustainability-led energy saving features, including a community heating system served by bio-diesel boilers and the use of wind turbines, have been incorporated into the design for Larden Road. Reinforcing the benefits of these measures with high quality passive design features, significant attention has been given to the integrity of the overall building envelope across the development; wall insulation exceeds standard building requirements throughout the scheme and optimising the orientation of each building for natural light capture, temperature control and energy efficiency, none of the homes have principal aspects that are solely north-facing. Genesis conducted a lifetime cost analysis on specifications throughout the development and construction materials were all chosen with consideration of their sustainable value. Accompanied

more generally by recycling facilities and features supporting environmentally friendly transport solutions, the proposals for Larden Road have gained the project a prospective Eco-Homes rating of 'very good'.

Meeting similarly high space standards, and exemplifying the potential for viable family housing within an affordable urban setting, Larden Road incorporates a large number of three bedroom family-sized apartments featuring separate kitchen and dining rooms, increased floor area and, heightening the natural lighting and perception of spaciousness, the provision of large windows, gardens and balconies to all affordable homes. Privately owned ground level units are arranged to front the street and have individual entrances while ten per cent of homes have been designed for wheelchair use. On the west-facing mixed-use blocks designed by bptw, residential spaces, located on the upper floors of the buildings have been structurally and visually separated from the ground level commercial spaces through the use of recessed levels. Similarly, full-height glazing for the commercial spaces contrast with the detailed brickwork, colourful rendered panels and timber balconies of the residential areas on the upper floors.

All communal amenities are located at ground level to provide accessibility and to emulate a traditional community streetscape; reinforcing the interaction

Opposite: A visualisation of the Cobbold Road entrance to the Larden Road scheme, the health centre is below residential units. *Above*: A massing model illustrating the blocks designed by bptw partnership.

between the commercial and residential features of the urban realm and encouraging the interactivity and industriousness of local residents. Allowing for adaptation to changing business needs, commercial spaces have been designed to an open plan and flexible layout, arranged around the residential buildings in such a way as to create a distinct focus point in terms of its sense of enclosure, familiarisation and orientation.

Providing for a large central open space amenity area, situated between two main residential blocks, accommodating an outdoor seating area in addition to commercial units and a cafe, and two smaller more passive landscaped areas, Larden Road comprises three distinct geometric components, internally linked with a pedestrian and vehicular thoroughfare that runs through the scheme providing an effective transport connection and an active commercial and residential frontage.

In contrast with the strong features of the centre of the development, the northern part of the scheme features a large green landscaped area with undulating levels and scales of planting. Incorporating children's play facilities and open community recreation space, the alternative cues for use indicated in this space epitomise the diversity of community provision required within a successful mixed-use development. Due for completion in 2010, the redevelopment of Larden Road will further

serve to highlight the community revitalisation that can be achieved through successful and strategically designed mixed-use development, particularly one where residents can live and work locally; specifically highlighting a return to the principles of a localised economy and the communal social and economic development of individual neighbourhoods as fundamental building blocks of wider urban living.

Opposite top: Elevation of Warple Way on the west-facing side of the site. *Opposite bottom*: A hand drawn concept sketch of designs for the development. *Above*: Visualisation of the cafe on the corner of the main central open space within the residential development.

Tottenham Town Hall

An exemplar project facilitating the regeneration of an important historic site in the heart of Tottenham, bptw were appointed as architects on the refurbishment of the Grade II listed Tottenham Town Hall, together with the wider mixed-used regeneration for the whole of the site in 2007.

In response to a competition run by Haringey Council, bptw were invited to tender development proposals for the site as part of a consortia led by Newlon Housing Trust in partnership with United House Ltd. Following their successful appointment, the winning proposals were subsequently put forward to an extensive public consultation process which took place in December 2007, for which the consortia produced a comprehensive exhibition outlining their development process, design proposals and their individual response to the history and context of the site.

Despite the highly positive initial response to the proposal consultation, the cultural significance of the site and its prominence in the local area inevitably led to a degree of controversy over some aspects of the scheme; notably concerning the removal of a former air raid shelter on the site, plans for the integration of the residential elements and the extent to which the Town Hall's original structure would be preserved in the process of accommodating the residential scheme. Significant changes to the initial proposal were subsequently developed before the final design was adopted.

Working with Newlon Housing Trust's regeneration team, Newlon Fusion, the Town Hall will be revitalised and become a single building focus for the third sector in the North London area. This will be closely linked with the extensive regeneration of Tottenham Hale where Newlon are also partners in a larger regeneration project, whilst providing an attractive and meaningful resource for the local community. Scheme designs will also preserve the unique historical character of the Grade II listed Town Hall and be developed with sensitivity to the David Adjaye designed Bernie Grant Arts Centre, a new iconic cultural hub situated immediately adjacent to the site.

Consultation and close liaison with English Heritage formed an integral part of bptw's design proposals, significantly informing the practice's strategy for the redevelopment of the Town Hall building and the transformation of its internal disused offices into space to accommodate new activities. Sympathetic to the building's historical heritage, the practice acknowledged and outlined the preservation of the Town Hall's most unique features, incorporating into the development proposals the restoration of the former Council Chamber; the Moorish-Jacobean Moselle room;

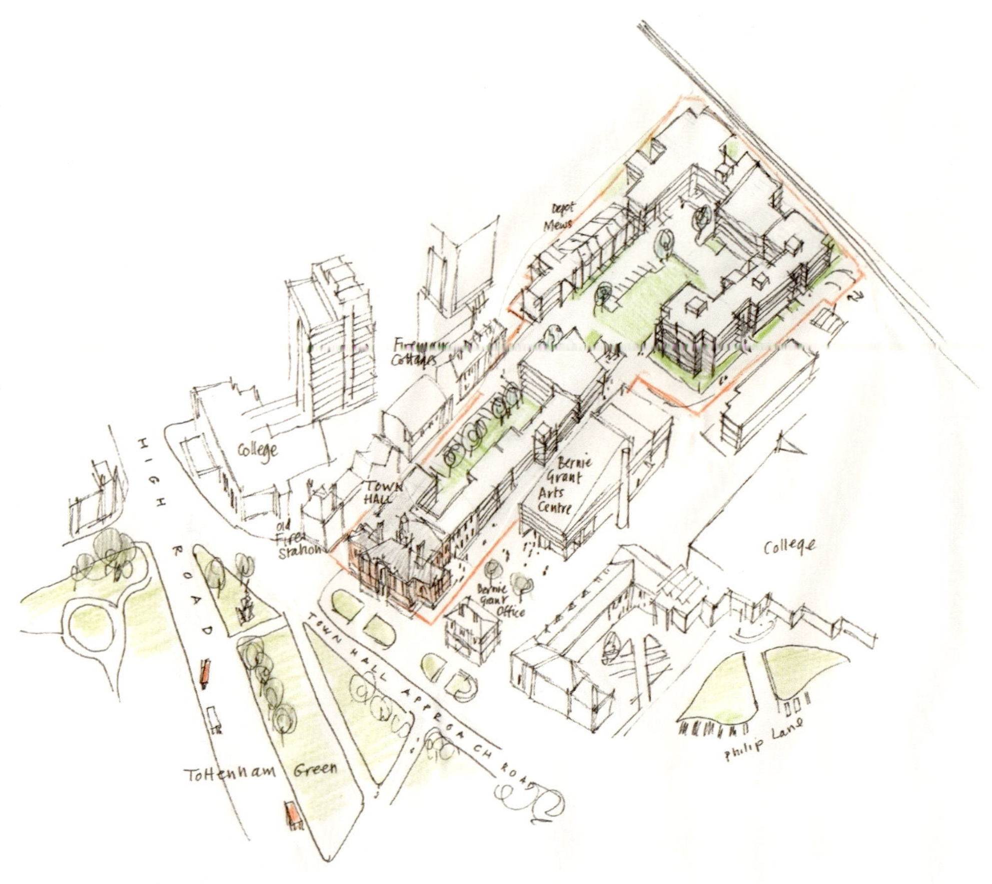

Opposite top: The marble staircase (pictured) at the centre of the existing town hall is just one of the listed features to be preserved as part of the redevelopment process.
Opposite bottom: Tottenham Town Hall, Tottenham.
Above: View of the existing Town Hall overlooking Tottenham Green.

the grand staircase and galleried landing, the main entrance with its attractive mosaic tiled floors and the front and side facades which were built from red brick and Portland Stone.

Complementing the historical and surrounding architectural context of the site, the residential solution consists of 107 spacious residential units and houses for affordable rent and private and shared ownership. Situated on the car park to the rear of the Town Hall and the adjacent dilapidated Clyde Road depot site, the scheme is divided into two large squares, one arranged to address the original Fireman's Cottages and the other around the central range of depot buildings which are being fully restored. The units are orientated for aspect and optimum solar gain and feature energy efficient services for power generation in line with the sustainability strategy for the scheme.

More widely, the landscaped communal squares and thoroughfares clearly define the pedestrian-orientated public and private realm of the Tottenham Town Hall site, encouraging a vibrant and active shared streetscape. In accordance with Secured by Design standards, well-lit pathways to the squares are all designed to be overlooked by homes on the site, creating a distinct sense of community within the new residential development. Links to surrounding green spaces, cycle routes and transport interchanges in the neighbouring area have also been enhanced throughout the site.

Opposite top: 3-D initial concept model of the site at night.
Opposite bottom: Elevation across the site, illustrating the connection between the Town Hall, the new build homes and the existing public buildings.
Above: Sketch of the open space (and its prospective view as a functioning social hub) between the Town Hall and the housing designed to the rear of the site.

Timeline

1988–1992

- Mark Bottomley, Stephen Palmer, Roger Taylor and Alan Wright launch a new practice, Bottomley, Palmer, Taylor and Wright, Architects & Quantity Surveyors.
- The practice is appointed for its first major job at St George's & St Patrick's Court in the London Borough of Waltham Forest.
- The practice receives DTI grant funding for marketing, communications and business practice.
- The practice is appointed to carry out the extensive refurbishment of Bishport Avenue, Bristol.
- The practice changes its name to BPTW Architects and Quantity Surveyors.
- Founding partner, Stephen Palmer retires.

1993–1998

- bptw is appointed as masterplanner for the regeneration of the Woodpecker Neighbourhood at the Milton Court Estate in New Cross.
- Launch of the Single Regeneration Budget Challenge Fund by Michael Heseltine, former Secretary of State for the Environment.
- Launch of the Estate Renewal Challenge Fund.
- bptw is appointed as joint masterplanner for the regeneration of the Five Estates in Peckham.
- New Labour is elected at the General Election, led by Tony Blair.
- Launch of the *Rethinking Construction* report by the construction task force commissioned by former Deputy Prime Minister, John Prescott.
- bptw is appointed to a large stock transfer and regeneration of four estates in Charlton.
- Future partners; Bob Silcock, Mark Waite, Anna Parkinson, Andrew French, Andy Heath and Dave Welsh join the practice.

1999–2004

- Launch of the Millennium Commission's £2 billion investment in National Lottery projects.
- Andrew French becomes the first non-founding partner.
- Green paper "Quality and Choice: A Decent Home for All" led by former Deputy Prime Minister, John Prescott is published.
- bptw is appointed as masterplanner for the Pepys Estate in Deptford.
- bptw undertakes the masterplanning and design of the Elmington Estate in Camberwell.
- bptw gains Investors in People accreditation.
- Partner, Roger Taylor retires.
- Anna Parkinson, Dave Welsh and Bob Silcock become partners.
- bptw partnership opens a second office in Epping, Essex.
- Housing Corporation's Challenge Fund is established.
- Former Deputy Prime Minister, John Prescott launches the Decent Homes Target Implementation Plan and the Sustainable Communities Action Programme.
- Logic Homes (formerly known as Gentect) is launched.
- The London Wide Initiative is launched.
- Housing Corporation's Challenge Fund II is launched.
- bptw is appointed for the stock transfer feasibility and later the regeneration of the former Sundermead Estate in Lewisham, now known as River Mill Park.
- The practice is listed in the Sunday Times 100 Best Small Companies to Work For.
- Future partner, Carol Strevens joins the practice.

2005–2008

- bptw takes part in, and receives commendation in the Design for Manufacture Competition to design a £60K house.
- bptw wins two CABE Standard for Life Awards for Elmington Estate and Pepys Estate.
- bptw partnership wins Building Magazines 'Architectural Practice of the Year'.
- Partner Dave Welsh retires.
- bptw launches its visualisation service.
- Andy Heath, Mark Waite and Carol Strevens become partners.
- bptw designs phase one of a new build development in a prominent position overlooking the river Thames at Greenwich Wharf, Greenwich.
- bptw is appointed as architects alongside Logic partner, SHP and Living Architects to design a new build residential development in Larden Road, Acton.
- The Code for Sustainable Homes is launched and replaces Eco-Homes.
- Prime Minister, Gordon Brown announces bid to build three million new homes by 2020.
- bptw celebrates its twentieth anniversary.
- bptw launches its new planning service.
- Home Communities Agency launched.

Selected Bibliography

- Hanley L, *Estates—An Intimate History*, London: Granta Books, 2007.
- Jacobs J, *The Death and Life of Great American Cities*, London: Jonathon Cape, 1962.
- Schumacher EF, *Small is Beautiful*, London: Abacus Ltd, 1974.
- Sennett R, *The Fall of Public Man*, London: Faber & Faber, 1986.
- Sherlock H, *Cities are good for us*, London: Paladin, 1991.
- Newman O, *Defensible Space—People and Design in the Violent City*, London: Architectural Press, 1972.
- Newman O, *Design Guides for Creating Defensible Space*, London: Architectural Press, 1976.
- Vale B and R, *Green Architecture: Design for a Sustainable Future*, London: Thames and Hudson, 1991.

Acknowledgements

We would like to thank Nick Raynsford MP for providing the foreword and gratefully acknowledge his ongoing support of our industry. Rachel Snook assimilated the research and drew together the text for the book and Catherine Muckle managed the production of the project, assisted by Lucy Herdsman. Aspects of this book would not have been possible without the help of Samantha Holmes and Dean Wells who enabled us to obtain and archive the images we required and Lyndal Stuart, who first developed the concept of this book and established our initial liaison with Black Dog Publishing. We thank Chris Johnson, Archie Russell and Ian Jones for their invaluable input on Milton Court and Peckham Partnership. Peter Kent created the topographical sketches for our case studies and photography is courtesy of Robert Greshoff, Tim James, David Millington, Paul Tanner, David Stewart and Daniel Jarvis. We are very grateful to Duncan McCorquodale and his team for their support and guidance throughout. Lastly, we thank our staff and clients, past and present, who have enabled us to become the practice we are today and made this publication worthwhile.

Index

£60k House **94, 187**
Aalto, Alvar **7**
Abode, Harlow **162**
Adjaye, David **182**
Affordable Home Ownership Awards **126**
Alfred McAlpine **29**
Allenbuild Ltd **91**
Alsop, Will **57**
Approved Development Programme **91**
Aragon Tower Block **114**
Architectural Practice of the Year **83**
Arms Length Management Organisations **85**
Avenue Road, Leytonstone **12**
Axis Development **86, 91**
Badcock's Wharf **168**
Basildon **31, 153, 162–163, 165**
Battersea **119, 132–133**
Battersea Park **133**
Battersea Power Station **133**
Beaver Housing Society **29**
Bentham Court, Islington **29**
Berkeley Homes **114**
Bernie Grant Arts Centre **182**
Best Companies List **83**
Bishport Avenue **10, 22–23, 25, 46, 186**
Blair, Tony **196**
Blyth and Blyth **173**
Botes Building **78**
Bottomley, Mark **7, 13, 186**
Bottomley, Palmer, Taylor & Wright, Architects and Quantity Surveyors **7, 9–10, 13, 186**
Bow **91**
Brick Awards **96, 114**
Bristol City Council **22, 24**
Brown, Gordon **147, 187**
Building for Life **114**
Building Magazine **10, 18, 22, 83, 187**
CABE Award **83**
Camberwell **36, 55, 96, 98–99, 187**
Catford Stadium **86**
Catherine Grove **86, 91**
Challenge Fund **27–28, 33, 35, 50–51, 58, 85, 91, 70–72, 153, 162, 186–187**
Charlton Church Lane **35**
Charlton Triangle **33, 35, 70, 71, 72, 73, 74, 75**
Charlton Triangle Homes Housing Association **35**
Chelsea Power Station **149**
Chingford Hall **29**
Circle 33 Housing Trust **32, 122, 126**
Circle Anglia Housing Association **29, 91**
City Challenge **27**
Clinton House **29**
Clyde Terrace **150, 154, 156–161**
Code for Sustainable Homes, The
Commission for Architecture and the Built Environment (CABE) **152, 187**
Communities Plan **147**
Community Safety Award **48**
Connaught Construction **24**
Construction Task Force **33, 186**
Convoy's Wharf **119**
Copper Point **91, 93**
Countryside **53, 86, 91, 98**
Coutts House **35, 71–72, 75**
Continuing Personal Development (CPD) **152**
Cranes Farm Road, Basildon **53, 91, 153, 162–165**
Crank's Restaurant **12**
Cranwood Street **11**
Crawley **90–91**
Decent Homes Standard **85**
Deptford **29, 96, 114, 150, 187**
Design for Homes **152**
Design for Manufacture **94, 187**
Diamond Build **110**
Donnybrook Quarter **86, 91**
Department of Trade & Industry **13, 186**
Durkan Group, The **91**
EC Harris **156**
East Greenwich **13, 149, 168, 173**
Eco-Homes **120, 133, 141, 149, 162, 173, 178, 187**
Edrich House **33–34**
Egan, Sir John **33, 94**
Elmington **83, 96–103, 187**
English Heritage **115, 119, 182**
English Partnerships **94, 162**
Environment Agency **139**
Epping **86, 187**
Erith **93–94**
Estate Action **7–8, 22, 28, 33, 38–39, 42, 51, 114, 116**
Estate Renewal Challenge Fund **33, 35, 58, 70, 72, 85, 186**
Evelyn Court **114**
Family Housing Association **33, 35, 53, 70**
Farrell & Partners **149**
Farrer Huxley Associates **176**
Finchley Methodist Church **12**
Five Steps Nursery **104–109**
Forest Hill Urban Design Framework **156**
French, Andrew **31, 186–187**
Galliford Hodgson **46, 72**
Gaumont House **37**
Genesis Housing Group **91, 149, 162, 166, 176**
Gibney, Mark **150**
Great Billing Way **153**
Greater London Authority (GLA) **177**
Greenwich **5, 13, 37, 70, 86, 91, 168, 173, 187**
Greenwich Millennium Village **173**
Greenwich Wharf **147, 149, 153, 168–175, 187**
Hammarby Sjostad, Stockholm **152**

Handcroft Road Estate **29, 36, 46–49**
Haringey Council **182**
Haringey Design Awards **110**
Hartcliffe, South Bristol **10**
Hatfield Close, Lewisham **78–79, 81**
Hawke Tower **28–29, 40, 43**
Heath, Andy **31, 186–187**
Heseltine, Michael **27, 186**
Higgins Construction **104**
Higgins Homes **91**
Hill Partnerships **91**
Hilton's Wharf **37**
Homes Communities Agency **187**
Home Zone **96, 121, 142, 144, 153, 162–163**
Hoey, Kate **58**
Housing Corporation **91, 94, 147, 162, 187**
Housing Corporation Scheme Development Standards **133, 141**
Housing Design Awards **96, 114**
Housing Design Conference **147**
Hunt Thompson Associates (HTA) **9**
Hunters & Partners **86**
Hyde Housing Association **33, 53, 96, 114–115**
Hyde Southbank **58**
Investors In People **83, 94, 187**
J Hodgson Ltd **16**
John Laing Partnership **62, 138, 142**
Joseph Tritton **119, 132–135**
JUNP (Joining up Northumberland Park) **110**
Kender **76–81**
Kender Estate **76, 80**
Kender Triangle **76**
Laing Partnership Housing **53**
Land Use Consultants **173**
Larden Road **149, 153, 176–181, 187**
Laurels Healthy Living Centre **85, 122–123, 126–127**
Legendary Property Company (LPC) **128**
Leven Road, Poplar **150**
Levitt Bernstein **9**
Lifetime Home Standards **100, 119–120**
Lifetime Homes **65, 141, 168**
Lime Tree House **27, 31–32, 62–67, 79**
Living Architects **176, 187**
Lloyd Wright, Frank **7**
Logic Homes **91, 94, 149, 153, 162, 166, 176, 187**
London & Quadrant Housing Trust **136, 138**
London & Regional Properties **149, 168**
London Borough of Barking and Dagenham **86**
London Borough of Croydon **29, 46**
London Borough of Greenwich **33**
London Borough of Hammersmith and Fulham **149, 176**
London Borough of Haringey **7, 110, 122, 126**
London Borough of Lambeth **33**
London Borough of Lewisham **13, 27, 38–39, 76, 79–80, 86, 104, 114, 136, 138, 156–158**
London Borough of Southwark **51, 55, 62, 96, 98**
London Borough of Waltham Forest **9, 14, 186**
London Borough of Wandsworth **132**
London Renewables Toolkit **152**
London Wide Initiative (LWI) **86, 91, 187**
Lots Road **149**
Lough Road **91**
Lymington Fields **85–86**
Mabley Green **32–33**
Manchester City Centre **128, 130**
Manchester Ship Canal **128**
Mansell Construction **46**
Maritime Greenwich **173**
Mayor of London **149**
Maze Hill School **86**
McCann Homes **91**
Metropolitan Police **53**
Millennium Commission **85, 187**
Millennium Dome **173**
Milton Court Estate **13, 38, 186**
Milton Court Masterplan **28, 42**
Modern Methods of Construction **94, 120, 162, 166,**
National Housing Federation **126**
National Lottery projects **85, 187**
National Science Museum **151, 153**
NDC **80, 122**
Neighbourhood Wardens **110**
Netherlands, The **65**
New Cross Gate **80**
New Cross **38, 76, 186**
Newlon Housing Trust **110, 182**
NHS Primary Care Trust **86**
Northumberland Park Neighbourhood Resource Centre **110–113**
Oliver Close **29**
Open House London **110**
Orbit Group **94**
Ordsall Estate **128–131, 155**
Ordsall Hall **130**
Palmer, Stephen **7, 13, 186**
Parkinson, Anna **31–32, 83, 186–187**
Peckham **27, 36–37, 50–51, 53–54, 57, 59, 63, 79, 186**
Peckham library **57**
Peckham Partnership **27, 31, 35–36, 50–57, 62, 96, 98, 149, 188**
Peckham Pulse **57**
Peckham Traders Association **53**
Pepys **96–97, 114–121, 133, 139, 161, 171**
Pepys Estate **96, 114–115, 119, 121, 187**
Pepys Estate Action **116**
Phippen, Randall & Parkes **9**

Pipers Wharves **168**
Pollard Thomas Edwards Architects (PTEa) **7, 27, 51, 53, 98**
Polychrome Court, Waterloo **90, 91**
Poundbury **162**
Prescott, John **33, 85, 94, 147, 186–187**
Presentation: Social Investment Agency **53**
Primrose Hill **12**
Private Finance Initiative **85**
Raynsford, Nick **5, 188**
Radburn principles **29, 46**
Rethinking Construction **33, 186**
River Irwell **130**
River Mill Park **94, 96, 136–145, 187**
River Ravensbourne **95, 138–140, 144**
River Thames **96, 115–116, 169, 172–174, 187**
Robin Hood Gardens **5**
Rotherhithe **91**
Royal Borough of Kensington and Chelsea **149**
Royal Festival Hall **147**
Royal Institute of British Architects (RIBA) **152**
Rydon Construction **97, 115**
Salford City Council **128**
Salford Quays **128, 130**
Sampson Associates **7, 11**
Scharoun, Hans **7**
Science of Survival exhibition **151, 153**
Secured by Design Standards **183**
Sheppard Robson **7**
Shepway Estate, Maidstone **29**
SHP **91, 176, 187**
Siege House **94**
Silcock, Robert **31, 83, 186–187**
Silwood Community Centre **108**
Silwood Estate **104**
Silwood Pocket Park **104**
Single Regeneration Budget (SRB) **27–28, 36, 51, 98, 104, 186**
SOLFED **53**
Southwark Park **91, 93**
Squire and Partners **168–169**
St. George's Court **8, 14–21, 186**
St. Patrick's Court **8–9, 14–21, 186**
Strevens, Carol **152, 187**
Stockwell **33–34, 58**
Studley Community Centre **58–60**
Studley Estate **33–34, 59**
Sunday Times 100 Best Companies to Work For **83**
Sundermead Estate **94, 96, 135, 138, 142, 144, 187**
Sure Start **110**
Swan Housing Group **150**
Talbot Road, Northampton **166–167**
Taylor, Roger **7, 83, 186–187**
Tengbomgruppen Architects **152**
Thames Gateway **91**
Thatcher, Margaret **7**
The Bridge NDC **122**
Threshold Housing **132**
Tottenham Hale **182**
Tottenham Town Hall **182–185**
Tottenham, North London **94, 110, 122**
Tower Hamlets Community **94**
Tower Homes **136, 138**
Tramway House **93–94**
Tushmore Roundabout and Spire **90–91**
Tweeds Construction Consultancy **173**
United House Ltd **182**
Urban Renaissance Scheme **136**
Volumetric units **93**
Waite, Mark **31, 151, 186–187**
Waltham Forest Housing Action Trust **29**
Wapping **94**
Warple Way **181**
Watermill Court **138, 142**
Wates Construction **46**
Watkins Gray International LLP **86**
Welsh, Dave **31, 186–187**
Wheelchair Housing Design Guide **141, 143**
White House, The **76, 78–81**
Willmott Dixon LLP **91**
Woodpecker Neighbourhood **13, 28, 38–40, 186**
Wright, Alan **7, 147, 186**

Black Dog Publishing Limited
10a Acton Street
London WC1X 9NG
United Kingdom

Tel: +44 (0) 20 7713 5097
Fax: +44 (0) 20 7713 8682
info@blackdogonline.com
www.blackdogonline.com

Designed by Julia Trudeau Rivest and Matthew Pull at Black Dog Publishing.

ISBN 978 1 906155 421

British Library Cataloguing-in-Publication Data.
A CIP record for this book is available from the British Library.

Black Dog Publishing Limited, London, UK, is an environmentally responsible company. *Celebrating Differences* is printed on Fedrigoni Symbol Freelife Satin, an environmentally-friendly ECF (Elemental Chlorine Free) woodfree paper with a high content of selected pre-consumer recycled material.

Printed in Italy by Servizi Tipografici Carlo Colombo s.r.l. - Rome

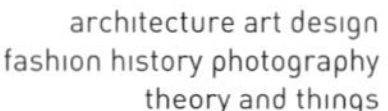